JTHE
JAPANESE

The Often Misunderstood, Sometimes Surprising, and
Always Fascinating Culture and Lifestyles of Japan

J THE JAPANESE

The Often Misunderstood, Sometimes Surprising, and
Always Fascinating Culture and Lifestyles of Japan

Jack Seward

Printed on recyclable paper

PASSPORT BOOKS
a division of *NTC Publishing Group*
Lincolnwood, Illinois USA

*The National Textbook
Company should not
encourage authors
who indulge
in the sort
of thing
we read in the chapter
on crime and punishment*

Library of Congress Cataloging-in-Publication Data

Seward, Jack.
   The Japanese / by Jack Seward.
     p. cm.
   Previously published: Tokyo, Japan : Yohan Publications, 1971.
   ISBN 0-8442-8393-2 (paper)
   1. Japan—Social life and customs—1945- 2. National
characteristics, Japanese. I. Title.
   [DS822.5.S3897 1992]
   952.04—dc20   92-8578
                                               CIP

1995 Printing

Published by Passport Books, a division of NTC Publishing Group,
4255 West Touhy Avenue, Lincolnwood (Chicago) IL 60646-1975 U.S.A.
©1992, 1971 by Jack Seward.
Manufactured in the United States of America.

  5 6 7 8 9 0 VP 9 8 7 6 5 4 3

For My Mother, Who Has Just Passed
Her 95th Birthday.

Contents

First Acquaintance with the Japanese

Time—treacherous, as always—had played another of its cruel tricks in passing far more quickly than it had any right to.

Counting the years as I was leaving for my home in the U.S., I was amazed to find that the total was twenty-five: almost half my life, nearly *all* of my adult life spent in six Japanese cities and towns as a writer, businessman, Army officer, and intelligence agent.

From the day of my arrival in Yokohama shortly after the close of the war in the Pacific, I had tried to live completely in the Japanese style, at some times in one cramped room and at others in a small, flimsy house with a single hibachi for both heating and cooking. I rode the incredibly crowded subways, trains, and buses to work and ate mostly Japanese food. I listened only to programs in Japanese on the radio, associated mostly with Japanese, and read Japanese newspapers and magazines more frequently than periodicals in English.

These things I did deliberately, although my preferences might sometimes have dictated otherwise, because I believed this was the only way by which I could ever achieve a significant understanding of all that Japan is: by simply being a part of it and letting it sink in.

After twenty-five years of this kind of life I went back to the small town in north Texas that is my family home, where the contrast between what had (and had not) happened there and what had happened in Japan during those years was extreme and unsettling.

If anything, my home town had retrogressed, although I must say I sometimes prefer such retrogression to what passes these days under the guise of progress. The population had declined. Most young people were moving away soon after graduation from high school. Businesses were decreasing in both number and scale. Television and the automobile had completely changed the style of social life, for the worse. While land prices were increasing, the rate was painfully slow: land values had not even doubled in twenty years—in sharp contrast to Japan, where increases of several hundredfold were not at all uncommon.

In Japan the movement had been forward, at breathtaking speeds. When I first passed through the southern sections of Tokyo after the war, I wondered in bemusement if this were not an agricultural district devoted entirely to the cultivation of just one crop, a crop called rubble— rubble that sprouted profusely in all directions, adorned here and there by a rusty safe that alone told the previous whereabouts of a now-pulverized shop or office.

Now the pendulum has swung a long, long way in the opposite direction. The Japanese have wrought history's most amazing national economic recovery, and wrought it largely with their own skills and energy, though backed by more than a little American aid and direction.

My acquaintance with Japan, however, did not begin in 1945 with the arrival of my transport ship in Yokohama harbor. Rather, it started six years before that in a far less likely location: a cattle ranch near Bartlesville, Oklahoma, where I was working during summer vacations from college.

The ranch owner was an oilman whose staff included two Japanese valets. I've long since forgotten their family names, but Henry and Dan taught me—against their better judgment, I suspect—a magnificent array of at least twelve Japanese words, mangled perhaps by my Texas-Oklahoma drawl. Why I badgered them for this knowledge, I don't remember.

I would like to think I was inspired by a premonition of things to come, but it was more likely just the curiosity of a country boy in initial contact with envoys from the Mysterious Orient.

Anyway, college classes resumed and the war started, and then in early 1943, Howard Van Zandt, an American recently repatriated from Japan, began teaching spoken Japanese at the University of Oklahoma. As my schedule wasn't too crowded, I elected to take the course. In the meantime, I had signed up for the Enlisted Reserve Corps and was called to active duty in the Army just as my first semester of Japanese studies was ending.

Six months in the infantry gave me a lot of other things to think about besides the Japanese language, so it was with considerable—and grateful—amazement that I learned one day a keen-eyed records clerk had spotted my one-semester course in that language on my college transcript and I was to be transferred to a Japanese language school sponsored by the Army on the University of Michigan campus. Here I entered the first of what became a series of three Army schools that provided me with more than two years of intensified training, first in the written and spoken language of Japan, then in its history, economy, geography, literature, and social structure.

This schooling came to a close in 1945, and we graduates were commissioned and sent to the Pacific Theatre and then to Japan to staff military government and assorted intelligence units under Douglas MacArthur's command.

In Japan I was struck, as almost all visitors are, by the many differences from my own country—differences that will be depicted in this book. Many of these distinctions and variances were immediately discernible, while others eased their way into my consciousness only after several months or even years.

But there was one most important difference of which I did not become fully aware until twenty-five years later, when I returned to the United States and found life-styles, at least around my home in Texas, to be comparatively relaxed, friendly, and pleasure-oriented. It was only then I began to realize fully the extent and the seriousness of the strains and stresses that living in Japan involves, both for long-term foreign residents and for the Japanese themselves.

Partly, I know, these strains and stresses stemmed from the fact that I was a Westerner trying to live as a Japanese in a society where even foreigners with twenty-five years of residence are treated (sometimes, admittedly, to their advantage) as if they had just got off the boat in Yokohama that very morning; but mostly they arose from the same factors that militate against the peace of mind of the Japanese themselves.

I recall, not so long ago, when Tokyo newspapers reported the results of an international survey sponsored by the Sanwa Bank, one of Japan's leading financial institutions. While granting it is difficult to accurately measure such factors as human happiness, this survey is nonetheless notable and interesting in what it suggests, if not proves. Selecting thirty-three contributing causes and conditions, such as longevity, working hours, crime, living space, wage levels, education, increased costs of living, old-age pensions, and public facilities, the survey then grouped these into six categories: social satisfactions, working conditions, personal satisfactions, presence or absence of irritant factors, safety and a sense of security, and the feeling of worthwhile living.

Assigning a base figure of 100 to Japan, the surveyors gave the United States top listing in this welfare and happiness index with a rating of 253. Great Britain followed with 213, then West Germany with 190, and France with 187.

Japan's overall low rating (it suggests the Japanese are less than half as happy as Americans) derived principally from such irritant factors as pollution, traffic congestion, lack of parks and public libraries, shortage of paved roads, inadequate drainage and sewage systems, commuting problems, soaring prices, population congestion, and varied serious neuroses arising from tense preoccupation with individual image and stance on the social scene.

With this background, it is hardly surprising to find another survey (based on a poll of 8,429 junior high-school students taken by the Japan Emigration Service not long after that) concluding that 46 percent of such students throughout Japan "would rather live in a foreign country than spend their lives in tradition-bound, feudalistic Japanese society."

The Japanese have paid a high price for their success. To fully comprehend just how high this price has been, one needs to draw upon the experience of living in Japan as most Japanese live. He needs to experience—or observe at first hand—the toil required in merely getting to and from his work-place, the tensions in a society where deviations from the norm earn looks of dismay and words of reproach, the abnegation of self on the altar of company loyalty, the frustrations of young educated women in finding rewarding jobs they are qualified to do, and the inadequate provisions for leisurely retirement.

Although Japan is our second-best customer (after Canada) and although we buy more from her than from any other country, little cultural or spiritual communion exists between our two countries, separated as we are by an abyss of incomprehension—that is deeper and more difficult to cross from our side than from theirs. For though it must be granted that it may be imperfect at times, their cumulative knowledge of us is much, much greater than ours of them. In illustration, consider this: Almost any Japanese can name at least five or ten of our states and five of our presidents besides the present one. How many Americans can name even one Japanese prefecture or prime minister?

Looked at in this light, the careful observer cannot regard the future of U.S.-Japan relations with the serene confidence that our security ties and the scale of our commerce would otherwise inspire. Obviously what is needed is an intensified effort at understanding.

I can only hope what follows will contribute to such understanding.

Land of the Ripe
Rice Ears

Whether the traveler approaches Tokyo from the direction of North America with the rising sun at his back or from Hong Kong and beyond with the setting sun to his left, he has a fair chance of viewing that Queen of Mountains, Fuji, depending upon the courtesy of the weather and the discourtesy of a polluted atmosphere.

If he fails to see the mountain in her awesome twelve-thousand-foot majesty, he can get another chance by taking any of the trains out of Tokyo for Nagoya, Kyoto, Osaka, Kobe, and beyond; all of these sweep down the coast past the foot of this extinct volcano which—with geisha and cherry blossoms—has too long and too simplistically characterized Japan to the Western world. And if he doesn't catch a glimpse of her even then, he would be well advised to content himself with a picture postcard showing the mountain.(One Japanese photographer has devoted his entire career to taking pictures of Mount Fuji from every possible angle and at all possible hours and seasons. This in itself is a revealing comment on the philosophy of Japanese art, in which the native artist does not try to innovate, to pioneer new art forms, but rather only to do better what others have already done before him—or what he himself has done before.)

No matter what part of Japan's geography the traveler is able to see from the window of his jet or train, three features will stand out: its greenness, its mountainous terrain, and its clear, fast rivers. Coming as I did from north Texas with

15

its monotonous flatness and muddy, sluggish streams, these three prominent features of the Japanese landscape made an indelible impression on me and are responsible, I am sure, for a considerable portion of the hold Japan has had on me for so long.

With more than three thousand islands, this archipelago—called *Nihon*, or "The Source of the Sun," by its people—extends along the eastern rim of the Asian continent from the northeast to the southwest for about 1,350 miles. At the closest points it is 124 miles from Korea and 186 from Russia. In area 140,000 square miles, it is not quite so large as California (an oft-used but nonetheless still useful comparison), which has only about one-sixth the number of people.

The four main islands of Honshu, Hokkaido, Shikoku, and Kyushu (in order of size) comprise 98 percent of the total area of Japan. The capital is Tokyo, located in central Honshu at about the same latitude as Fresno, Nashville, Newport News, and Seville.

With an abundance of evergreens, most of Japan's foliage remains verdant throughout the year, watered by reliable and plentiful rainfall and by the electricity-producing rivers and streams that rush down from the hills. Two parallel chains of mountains, broken here and there, follow the curve of the islands and occupy so much space that only 16 percent of the country is cultivated, although more than half of the land that slopes no more than 15 percent is tilled. (Irrigated rice is the principal crop, *Mizuho-no-kuni* or the Land of the Ripe Rice Ears being a literary name for Japan.)

Much of this tilled land centers around the large industrial areas of Tokyo-Yokohama, Nagoya, Kita-Kyushu, and Osaka-Kyoto-Kobe (these four contain about three-quarters of the country's population) as well as around Sapporo, Niigata, and Sendai. In terms of arable land and population, Japan leads the world with a density of nearly five thousand souls per square mile.

While its rivers are generally not navigable, no place in Japan is more than ninety miles from the open sea, whose waves beat against a coastline nearly 17,000 miles long. This coastline is more irregular along the Pacific coast of southern Honshu and western Kyushu, and provides many excellent harbors. Indeed, the lovely, island-dotted Inland Sea could accurately be called one mammoth harbor.

Hot springs and volcanoes are prominent features of the green landscape, there being 160 of the latter. Twenty of these have erupted during the twentieth century, but not Mount Fuji, whose last eruption was in 1707, when she covered Tokyo with six inches of volcanic ash.

Japan's climate is comparable to that of the eastern coast of North America from Nova Scotia south to Georgia, modified by continental and marine influences. The summers are humid, hot, and comparatively short. They start off with the major rainy season, brought by predominant winds that blow up from the Pacific on the south and east. Except for Hokkaido, the winters are mild and sunny, influenced by winds off the continental mass of Asia. One southbound ocean current—the Oyashio—cools northeastern Honshu, while the northerly-flowing Kuroshio warms the Pacific coast of the islands as far up as Tokyo. At Japan's northern tip, Hokkaido has four months of the year in which mean temperatures drop to below freezing, while on the southern island of Kyushu the climate is mild enough to permit two rice crops annually.

Such climatic distinctions constitute Japan's principal regional differences, the others mostly involving agricultural, fishery, and industrial products, dialects, traditional folk crafts, and certain local dishes.

Climate permitting, the airborne traveler should be able

to see, in addition to Mount Fuji, a good deal of Japan's capital city as his jet crosses over the city headed south or west.

The most arresting physical feature of Tokyo's low-lying urban sprawl is the orange-and-white Tokyo Tower, built in 1958 at a cost of $2,800,000 and visited by four million paying customers annually. At 1,092 feet, it is one of the tallest towers in the world. The city is not, however, noted for its high buildings, their statutory ceiling having been 102 feet, or about ten stories, until 1963.

High or low, this mass that sprawls out to the west and north of Tokyo Bay is one of the world's largest cities, a monstrous, teeming megalopolis at the northeast end of the 366-mile-long Tokaido (Eastern Sea Road) Corridor. Its "city tree" is the gingko, and its bird is the *yuri-kamome*, a species of sea gull. Within its boundaries can be found more than a hundred universities (plus ninety junior colleges) and nearly one-half of all the university students in Japan; the world's largest police force; five full-scale symphony orchestras; five hundred movie theaters; more than one thousand pachinko (pinball) parlors; three opera companies; 30,000 taxis (12,000 in New York); nearly one hundred newspapers; and three baseball parks, each drawing crowds of up to 45,000 nightly. This exuberant jumble of uncoordinated concrete construction is the center of the country's culture and of its commerce, where most success-oriented Japanese strive to live and long to thrive.

It is, above all else, a city of contrasts, of variety, of vitality, and of more than a little venery. Of renewal and almost reckless resurgence. Of nocturnal delights and daylight drive. Of rawboned excitement and drab ugliness and rare beauty and exotic quaintness. A city to be loved or hated but never ignored. . . .

When Westerners come to Tokyo to live, they usually experience a kind of cultural shock, a wrench of acclimatization varying in severity with the dissimilarity of their points of origin. They find themselves strained and unsettled by the turmoil, the tumult, and the never-ceasing clamor of cars and chaotic construction, of cabaret music, of Klaxons and swooshing jets and of the curious cacophony of sounds of the Tokyo night: the noodle peddler's flute, the clack-clack of clogs on the cement, the eternal barking and howling of the ubiquitous watchdogs, the sirens and fire engines and police patrols, the *blok-blok-blok* of the fire-watch as he signals "All's well!" by knocking his two sticks together, the rolling rumble of the shutters being shoved shut. They are angered or amused—or both—at absurd attitudes and accidents and antiquities. Their credulity challenged, they are puzzled and perplexed by peculiarities light years outside their ken. They are frustrated by language barriers and buffeted by the brusque urgency and hustle of pushing, prosperous, pulsating crowds. But in time the initial shock diminishes, becomes tolerable, and then these newcomers reach an individual compromise, an accommodation of life-styles with this, the earth's biggest, noisiest, most dynamic and contrast-packed human habitation.

Because there are no residential zoning regulations as we know them, you will find in Tokyo that the mansions of the affluent and mighty stand jowl to cheek with the sleazy stalls of fishmongers and miniature temples of exquisite beauty. And in the business district an ex-geisha may manage a 150-year-old *sushi* shop right next door to a brightly lit, chromeplated Kentucky Fried Chicken dispenser. You can take a picture of the ancient stone walls of the Imperial Palace and find soaring Tokyo Tower in the background. Undeniably disharmony has arisen from this attempt to blend the West with the East, but it is disharmony with a certain appeal, compounded of ever-changing patterns and sudden, unexpected green oases and charming retreats, of rickshaws and monorails, of the most subtly tasteful and the most blatantly meretricious.

It is a city where high-speed freeways let you glide low over rooftops, looking right into modern apartment bedroom windows and down on a tousled ancient network of narrow, jagged, ill-lit streets and flimsy native houses made of wood, bamboo, and paper, which in turn lie above the world's most advanced subway network. It is a city of elegant tea ceremonies and poetry-reading contests and geisha-graced banquets, of flower-arranging classes and compulsive viewing of cherry blossoms and polynational restaurants, of jarring rhythms and tattooed toughs and mad, lemminglike dashes for the sea in the summer. It is a delightful but bedeviling, intricately wrought mosaic that sprawls unique among the metropolitan centers of the world.

Within this one giant of a city are to be found the seven cosmopolitan areas of Shinjuku, Shibuya, Ikebukuro, Ueno, Asakusa, Gotanda, and Ginza, each of which is a respectable "city within a city." For example, one of the smaller ones—Ikebukuro—has 60 mah-jong parlors, 4 mammoth department stores, 120 hotels, 135 coffee shops, 436 bars, 27 cabarets, 19 theaters, 24 dancing schools, 191 restaurants of many types, 12 Turkish baths, 32 pachinko parlors, and 820 shops, 100 of which are underground. Shinjuku has even more of each, including the world's tallest hotel, a complex of subway stations through which two and a half million passengers pass each day, and plans for a tower that will stand 1,815 feet high (in contrast to the 1,092-foot Tokyo Tower).

The most overwhelming aspect of Tokyo is, of course, the prodigious number of people who live (if, indeed, *live* is the right word) within its borders: people in streams, clumps, masses, avalanches, floods, rivers, armies, hosts, and multitudes. Almost all of them have black hair and dark eyes, but there the similarity halts, for we see people ranging in shape, dress, and life-style from gigantic sumo wrestlers with topknots and in native dress to tiny, wizened old women stooped over almost double from long, arduous years in the rice paddies; from teen-age swingers to beggars with rented children; from golfing geisha to deaf shoeshine women; from financial magnates in Mercedes-Benz limousines to blind masseuses and masseurs being led down neighborhood streets at night by flute-blowing escorts; from the colorful but raucous *chindon-ya* (street bands) to begrimed ragpickers; and from harried housewives out for their afternoon shopping to the ubiquitous office workers in their white shirts and conservative suits.

Their numbers literally boggle the mind. The zeroes pile up in such rows that the eyes begin to lose touch with reality. Each of these men and women (and children) has a theoretical allotment of 0.4 square meters of living space, in contrast with 8.7 square meters in Paris, 9.2 in London, 11.9 in New York, and 45.2 in Washington, D.C. One block in the Sumida Ward of Tokyo holds the dubious honor of having the highest population density in the world, that of 24,320 persons per square mile, which is all the more remarkable when one considers that Sumida does not have many buildings over a few stories in height.

Dotted here and there across Tokyo's flat countenance are spots of greenery, the largest of these being the 250 acres that form the city's—and the nation's—spiritual heart: the low-lying, unobtrusive, mysterious Imperial Palace area, with its circumambient moat and massive fifteen-feet-thick stone walls that have stood and withstood for nearly four hundred years. Within these walls—but largely concealed from view by the many gnarled old pine trees—are the Imperial Household Ministry, a rice paddy, a biological research laboratory, bomb shelters, a chicken house, riding stables, tennis courts, garages housing Rolls-Royces and Mercedes-Benzes, and the Imperial Palace itself. In the days when it was called Edo Castle, the site was four or five times its present size, was protected by three moats, and was entered through one of thirty-six gates.

When Edo Castle was constructed in 1457, the waters of Tokyo Bay lapped at the base of its eastern battlements.

Other smudges of green on the metropolitan face are public parks (which are small in size and few in number) and private gardens, walled off from outside view and a world in themselves.

These gardens are a reflection of the reverence in which the Japanese hold nature and of their desire not to conquer it, as we try to do in the West, but to commune with it and, when necessary, submit to its demands. Depending upon the historical period in which they were developed, these gardens may be designed in any of several styles, such as the Shinden, Shoin, hill, castle, tea, and stroll. They eschew the formality and the utility of Western gardens and are carefully planned to appear completely *un*planned. They are the great outdoors in miniature, a distilled essence of nature where one can get away from the workaday world and confirm man's oneness with nature in quiet reflection.

While these "vignettes of nature" may be small, they are often constructed to appear larger when viewed from proper vantage points. The ends of paths and tiny streams, for example, are often concealed to give the impression that they extend much farther. Reflecting the Shinto belief that natural spirits exist in all things, much of the material used in their design is symbolic: the pine stands for longevity, the plum for beauty and esthetic perfection, the bamboo for pliable strength, and water for purification. In this way the garden may tell or at least suggest a story. And this story may vary somewhat with the viewer because only its barest outline is told, like that of a sailing ship vaguely sighted through the distant mist, leaving the viewer to fill in the details as suits his fancy.

Thus, the famous Ryoanji Temple Garden in Kyoto can be interpreted in at least two ways: its carefully raked sand and fifteen rocks in three groupings may be seen as islands in the sea or as mountain peaks emerging from the morning mist.

Japanese gardens are in themselves a mirror of the geography of Japan and the character of its people and their passion for understatement. Their spareness reflects the scarcity of arable land and mineral resources as well as the comparative poverty of the common people until recent years. Having done without for so long, the Japanese learned to make a little do in place of a lot. They learned to let one flower stand for a dozen, one tree for a forest, one pebble for a boulder. A hint was always better than a bold statement. A delicate color blended better with humility than bright reds and golds.

This principle was also followed in flower arranging, at which the Japanese excel. No need to place two dozen red roses in the tokonoma (alcove) in the living room when only one—enhanced by a green sprig of this and a brown twig of that—would do quite well by inviting the viewer's participation through use of his imagination. Also, the flower arrangements are often symbolic and as such are made up of three elements—*ten, chi,* and *jin,* or heaven, earth, and man—which inhibit profuse use of materials.

With land as costly as it is, not many Japanese these days can afford such gardens, so, in addition to such floral arrangements, they may also adorn their homes with bonsai and bonkei. The former are dwarfed trees (some only a foot high and five hundred years old) and the latter are miniature gardens in boxes, often incorporating bonsai. To men and women who have no gardens and who miss daily communion with nature, these carefully nurtured trees and box gardens offer some compensation.

There was much more greenery but far fewer gardens in Tokyo that day in 1456 when Dokan Ota started to build his castle there. Edo (Tokyo) was then nothing more than a mud flat with about one hundred houses and a clutch of largely indifferent peasants who amused themselves by watching whales cavort in the then-clear waters of the bay. Ota, however, was one of the early civic boosters. He looked at the vast, fertile Kanto Plain, the rivers watering it, the immense bay, the seven hills upon which future battlements and homes of the wealthy could be constructed, and the mild weather, and decided that with the right kind of promotion this wretched little hamlet might some day dominate the Kanto Plain. Or, his imagination really running riot, it might even advance so far as to become the central city of all of Japan, although he doubted, in soberer moments, that it would ever really be able to compete with the splendor of Kyoto off to the southwest.

Choosing as the site a place where an old fort had stood, Ota began to build his castle when he was but twenty-four years of age. Completed in April of the following year (1457 is generally accepted as Tokyo's birth date), the castle became the focal point of the prosperous community Ota went on to develop during the twenty-nine years of life remaining to him. In 1486, Sadamasa Uesugi—Ota's liege lord—became suspicious of his vassal's ambitions and arranged his assassination. After Ota's death, commerce declined, the castle fell into disrepair, and the inhabitants returned to their earlier lackadaisical ways.

One hundred years passed. In May of 1590, Hideyoshi— the five-foot-tall peasant-general and de facto ruler of Japan—was standing on a hill near Odawara, at the southern edge of the Kanto Plain, and looking to the north. He was there to lay siege to the mighty Odawara castle of the Hojo family. At his side stood Ieyasu Tokugawa, his second-in-command.

"When we defeat the Hojo clan, I shall give you this

region to administer as your own," Hideyoshi said to Tokugawa, who bowed in silent appreciation.

Hideyoshi thought for a moment, then asked: "From where will you govern these lands?"

"From here in Odawara, my lord," said Tokugawa, soon to be the founder of the dynasty that was to rule Japan for 264 years with a degree of strict control seldom achieved anywhere else in the world.

But Hideyoshi was both cautious and crafty. He knew that, after himself, Tokugawa was the most formidable military commander in Japan as well as an individual of vaulting ambition. If anything, he wanted Tokugawa even farther away than Odawara from his own stronghold in Kansai.

"No, not here," Hideyoshi said. "Build your bastion in Edo instead."

"Edo, my lord?" Tokugawa asked to be sure he had heard right. He was not at all enthusiastic, for he knew the half-ruined castle standing there at the edge of the mud flats.

Concealing his satisfaction, Hideyoshi nodded, then turned away from the still-kneeling Tokugawa.

Determined to make the best of a poor situation, Ieyasu Tokugawa had the old Edo castle torn down and, summoning some ten thousand laborers from the eight fiefs newly under his control, launched the construction of a larger, mightier castle, bringing the massive stones for the thick walls by ship from distant Hyogo and surrounding it with three deep moats two hundred feet wide in some places. Not long after the castle was completed, Hideyoshi died; and after some internal scuffling to see who would succeed him as the "Barbarian-Subduing Generalissimo," Tokugawa became, in 1603, the Shogun himself.

One of the first things he did—after putting down on paper a set of "House Laws" by which his descendants were to govern themselves and Japan for the next 264 years—was surely a stroke of administrative genius that was to shape the character of Edo—and present-day Tokyo—more than any other single factor. He instituted the system of *sankin-kōtai*.

It was brilliant in its simplicity but massively burdensome in what it demanded of others. Japan was then divided up among more than three hundred fiefs—feudal kingdoms of varying sizes ruled by daimyo, or territorial barons. The *fudai* daimyo were those closely allied to the Tokugawa house, while the *tozama* (or outer) daimyo were the more distant, sometimes hostile, and often powerful clan chieftains. Tokugawa had decided to order all of them to build residences in Edo and to spend part of each year there under the watchful eyes of his magistrates—and to leave their families behind as hostages during those months when they were back home attending to local affairs (and perhaps plotting his downfall, he thought darkly).

The foundation of what was to become this mighty metropolis was therewith accomplished by a few strokes of the *fude*. More than three hundred daimyo and eighty thousand of their samurai poured into the burgeoning city, together with their families and many of the most capable administrators from each fief. Large-scale construction was launched. Battalions of builders, then artisans and merchants, gathered. Persons long immured in the hinterlands were exposed to new tastes, fashions, pleasures, and philosophies. They wanted more—and there was always someone there to cater to their desires. Keenly aware of the unrelenting hostility of many of the outer daimyo, Tokugawa demanded of them ever-increasing expenditures on ceremonies, staff, shrine construction, and civic repairs— to keep their resources in a state of near-depletion.

He then decided that one Edo residence was not enough, that each daimyo should maintain two: one near at hand, so that the daimyo could be within easy fetching distance, and the other farther off, where most of his warriors would be stationed—outside the protective walls of the moat. Provincial revenues poured into Edo to cover these costs. Cash-and-credit finances replaced the rice-and-barter economy of the countryside. New ideas and odd sights stimulated the peoples who came into Edo in a steady stream. The city began to call itself *Ō-Edo*, or Great Edo, and took on the not-entirely-unjustified airs of a progressive, vigorous, and sophisticated city. In short, the city boomed.

And so it was throughout the 264 years of the so-called Tokugawa Era. While rural Japan toiled in the fields and rice paddies and slept—and, in many ways, stagnated—Great Edo continued to reign as the economic, cultural, political, and military heart-and-brains of Japan. There were, of course, setbacks, delays, detours, and distractions, but in general the movement was steady and forward. Against the background of the marvelous political stability of the Tokugawa there was enacted a continuing drama in which disastrous fires, assassinations, vendettas, and earthquakes figured strongly.

But in 1853, Commodore Matthew Perry's "black ships" anchored off Uraga, close to Yokohama, and presaged the downfall of the Tokugawa regime, which was already harassed by domestic discontent. Pressured by gunboat diplomacy into ratifying the unpopular foreign treaties, the last Tokugawa Shogun was forced by dissident elements into abdicating his de facto throne so that the way might be paved for the "Imperial Restoration" of 1868, the beginning of the new Meiji Era. The Emperor Meiji moved from Saikyo ("western capital"), or Kyoto, to Edo, took over Edo Castle as his residence and palace, and renamed the city Tokyo ("eastern capital").

The new emperor lost no time in seeing to it that his administration lived up to its ambitious name, "The Era of Enlightened Government." Gathering about him some of the most intelligent and farsighted young men in his realm, he decided that Japan would have to meet the Western world on its own terms. In order to do so, she would have to learn a great deal from the West, so foreign teachers, specialists, engineers, and consultants were invited to Japan in droves.

Displaying their talent for adaptability on an as yet untested scale, the Japanese decided that since they obviously could not beat the West, they would, if not join it, at least learn from it. They hoped, however, to avoid sinking to slavish imitation. They would regard the models held up for their consideration with a critical eye, accept or reject, and then, perhaps, alter those found acceptable to suit their own national character. They would follow the principle of *Wakon-yōsai* and blend the Japanese spirit with Western knowledge, just as they had done centuries before when they melded the Japanese spirit with Chinese learning (*Wakon-kansai*).

In this effort, Japan was blessed with the talented leadership of a group of extraordinary men who were farsighted, devoted, and brilliant: Ito, Okubo, Kido, Okuma, Itagaki, Iwakura, Inoue, and Yamagata. A group of men comparable, in several senses, to those who managed the American Revolution, wrote the Constitution, and steered the young republic through its unsteady infancy. These Japanese leaders traveled to Europe and to the United States to see for themselves the sources of the power that had produced Perry's black ships and the naval squadrons that had bombarded Kagoshima and Shimonoseki. They arranged for a continuing influx into Japan of Western teachers, experts, and technicians: Englishmen, who supervised the construction of a modern navy and the development of a system of coinage; Americans, who reformed the educational machinery and taught Western agricultural methodology; Frenchmen and Germans, who both contributed to the codification of Japanese law and the organization of a new army. And again, Germans, who directed the establishment and administration of medical schools.

Postal and telegraph systems, modern mining, national and international finance, development of harbors, paper mills, scientific laboratories, construction of modern office buildings and government edifices, sanitation, railroads, prison reform (including the abolition of torture), cotton mills, water works, steam-powered factories—all these and more were substantially the creations and contributions of Westerners employed and directed by Japan's leaders, who managed at the same time to stifle efficiently and thoroughly the strong opposition of those samurai who wanted to retain their two swords, top-knots, and sinecures as idle vassals of feudal lords, of those lords themselves who did not wish to relinquish the control of their fiefs to central authority, and of a varied lot assembled under the banner of "*Sonnō! Jōi! Sakō!*" (Revere the Emperor! Expel the barbaric Westerners! Close the ports!)

While this miracle of internal transformation was taking place, Japan was also displaying its newly acquired military prowess on the international scene. After unilaterally annexing Okinawa from China in 1872, she dispatched, in May of 1874, a force of three thousand samurai to Formosa to punish the natives there for killing several Okinawan sailors, and then forced the Chinese government to pay an indemnity and to admit the culpability of her Formosan subjects in the incident. In 1894–5, Japan fought her first major foreign war of the Meiji Era with China and won the island of Formosa, with its considerable natural resources, as spoils of her victory. But many Western observers regarded this as merely another internal squabble in Asia and did not consider Japan's victory as meaningful proof of her strength in a larger international arena. The proof they lacked was not long in coming. In 1904–5, Japan challenged Czarist Russia over spheres of influence on the continent of Asia and, by destroying the

Imperial Russian fleet at the Battle of Tsushima Strait with a classic crossing of the T, won the southern half of Sakhalin together with the respect, if not the friendship, of the world.

In 1910, only two years before the death of the Emperor Meiji, Japan annexed Korea. When the First World War came along like an encore to the Meiji drama, she sided with the Allied Powers, assisted the French in the Mediterranean, and saw minor military action in the Indian and Pacific Oceans, thereby securing for herself—at a cost of only three hundred men killed in battle—a position as one of the Big Five Powers and as one of the Big Three in terms of naval strength. As a bonus, Japan also earned a degree of prosperity that pushed her growing industry much farther along its path of competition with the West and that sowed some of the seeds of the disastrous ambitions that were to follow.

Hakkō ichiu is what they called the concept in Japanese: the eight corners of the world under one roof. For the somewhat less megalomaniacal, there was the *Dai-Tōa Kyōeiken*, or Greater East Asia Co-Prosperity Sphere. The successes of the Meiji, Taisho, and early Showa Eras had served to persuade many Japanese militarists, politicians, and industrialists that Japan's unique status as the Land of the Gods imbued her people with a charismatic quality that enabled—indeed, compelled—them to lead the less fortunate and often incomprehensibly recalcitrant races of the Far East to a better way of life, whether they wanted to be led or not.

As with Japan's previous era, the curtain on this one rose auspiciously enough, if somewhat slowly and fitfully. The Greater Japan National Essence Society (*Dai-Nihon Kokushi-kai*) was formed in 1919 and the National Foundation Society (*Kokuhonsha*) in 1924. In 1929, staff members of Japan's Kwantung Army arranged the murder of

Chang Tsolin, a Manchurian war lord, in an unsuccessful attempt to force their government into war with China. In 1931, Premier Hamaguchi was assassinated, and a military takeover of the government by a group of army officers (the *Sakura-kai*) and certain civilian extremists was barely averted. On September 18, 1931, without prior consultation with the Cabinet in Tokyo, the Kwantung Army arranged the Mukden Incident on the South Manchurian Railway and used this as a pretext to overrun Manchuria. In 1932, Premier Inukai was assassinated, spelling the end to party government in Japan. Other assassinations and incidents, such as those of the *Panay* and the Marco Polo Bridge, followed as the Thirties wore on.

Although in 1941 Japan was still far from conquering all of China, she controlled, albeit at times not so securely, enough of China's coast, industry, population, and major cities to earn respect for her boast that she would eventually dominate it all. On December 7, 1941, she threw all of her might into a series of military attacks and campaigns that encompassed the near-destruction of the U.S. Pacific Fleet and much of its finest naval facility away from the American mainland, the subjugation of Singapore (which British leaders had long boasted was impregnable), the sinking of the British battleships *Repulse* and *Prince of Wales* by air power, the capture of Hong Kong, the subdual of Corregidor, and the eventual conquest of the Philippines, Indonesia, Southeast Asia, and many Pacific islands, large and small.

The Japanese had risen high. Too high, as it turned out. And they had ridden roughshod over the backs of too many people. Their descent was, fittingly, more precipitate than their climb. After the cessation of hostilities and the signing of the surrender document aboard the battleship *Missouri* in Tokyo Bay, the Japanese lifted their heads to see their cities devastated, their property and wealth stripped from them, millions dead, and more millions homeless and hopeless. Few peoples had ever been so thoroughly beaten.

The problems they faced have been, by and large, solved. But having solved these, the Japanese of the late 20th century faced still another set of problems—admittedly less formidable than defeat, poverty, and starvation, but exasperating nonetheless because many of the new set were derived from success, prosperity, industrialization, Westernization, and technical advance.

How successful they will be in dealing with these new problems is impossible to predict, but it is a safe bet that the Japanese will tackle them with the same energy and ingenuity they have displayed in recent years.

Hot Springs and Baths

Despite nearly three years of concentrated study of the language and culture, we entered Japan shortly after the close of the Pacific war without knowing how really hot a Japanese bath can be. (Japan's hottest public baths are to be found in the resort town of Kusatsu, north of Karuizawa, where the temperature hovers around 120 degrees Fahrenheit and where professional bath-masters are employed to lecture first-time bathers on the safest way to enter the caldrons and who lead them in by the numbers, like army drill sergeants. During the first inundation, which is limited to only three or four minutes, the bath-masters hover over their submerged platoons shouting encouragement, cautioning all to remain still to lessen the searing effect on the skin, and counting off the seconds remaining until the blessed reprieve of surfacing. In Chamberlain's day, according to his *Things Japanese*, the bath-masters used trumpets to urge their foolhardy phalanxes in and out of the waters, but this practice is now passe, so perhaps progress is a word with some meaning, after all.)

Blissfully ignorant of such temperatures, two of my classmates and myself made a weekend trip shortly after arrival in Japan to the hot springs resort of Tsuetate in the mountains of central Kyushu. In those difficult days, there were not many Japanese guests in any of the inns, so we were largely on our own when we strolled into the spacious communal bathroom of our inn for the first time. One of my classmates, Huntley, lowered himself blithely into the inviting expanse of bath water and then climbed right back out again, only with much greater alacrity.

Aghast at his broken whimpering and the bright red hue of his lower parts, Bill and I were backing away from the pool-sized bath when the door opened and two maids of the inn entered, both mother-naked.

As I recall that scene today, I find it difficult to recognize myself therein, the intervening years and other sexually-desegregated baths having completely revised my fundamental thinking about such matters. I was then a twenty-one-year old Army lieutenant who had never before bathed in the buff with any woman whose name I did not at least know, but getting into the same bath toward which these two unconcerned and unclothed maids were obviously headed seemed somehow better than standing there face to face with much to conceal (at least in terms of epidermal area) but nothing to conceal it with.

After a few minutes of searing torture, Huntley saved the day by shouting "*Jishin da! Jishin da!*" (Earthquake! Earthquake!), whereupon the two maids fled with the same precipitate haste that we instantly emulated in getting out of that tub of thermal torment. (That most Japanese have a healthy and no doubt justified fear of earthquakes, we were already well aware. Their first compulsion is to instantly flee, like startled grasshoppers, to the great, roofless outdoors.)

Mirable dictu, Huntley quickly became a confirmed devotee of the Japanese bath: in particular, the Japanese communal bath. He soon began to spend his weekends in one or another of Kyushu's many hot springs, most of which are renowned for their therapeutic qualities. To explain away this sudden addiction, Huntley developed a case of instant arthritis, from which, he told the men and women in our unit, he was able to obtain remarkable relief during and after a weekend of heated immersion.

His true absorption, however, focused on the unlimited ogling opportunities thus provided, which he preserved for repetitive pleasures through the medium of photography. Cunningly, he learned to stroll nonchalantly into busy, bisexual baths with a towel draped over one arm to conceal the essence of his maleness and a 35 mm camera, cocked and loaded–for bare.

When the Japanese bathers had lost interest in his foreign presence, Huntley would artfully expose the lens of his candid camera and begin shooting from the hip with extraordinarily revealing results, which he would show to me on Thursday of each week, as soon as the film sent out the first thing Monday morning had been developed and printed in magnificent enlargements. He averaged taking one 36-exposure roll of very fast split-frame 35 mm film each weekend, or nearly three hundred shots monthly. About one-third of these turned out to be worthy of careful study, so Huntley began tacking them to the walls of his room, which others in the unit took to calling the Huntley Gallery. We all spent many pleasant hours there, wrapt in both above-and-below-the-navel contemplation.

Huntley's come-uppance came with the arrival of his American wife in one of the first shipments of dependents. The pictures posed no real problem: the Huntley Gallery merely became the Seward Gallery, and Huntley moved into his new dependent quarters with his wife Joy. The rub, however, was that everyone, including the WAC's, knew of the "medical necessity" for his weekly trips to *onsen* (hot springs), and he realized that it would be suspicious for him to announce a sudden, almost miraculous cure that coincided with his wife's appearance on the scene. There was no help for it. He would have to taper off gradually, over a period of several months, while occasionally remarking loudly on a further improvement in his arthritis.

So it came to pass that Huntley continued to visit his beloved hot springs—but with Joy, who was a statuesque blond and who appeared little, if any, daunted at the prospect. Indeed, I sometimes wondered if she did not sense the truth and welcome the opportunity to discomfit Huntley for his willingness to expose her, to avoid exposing his own errant ways.

At any rate, Huntley took his wife with him every weekend for three or four months, spreading unadorned Joy among a great number of Japanese men and perhaps thus compensating them for similar views vouchsafed him of their wives and daughters.

Bathing has deservedly been called The Grand Passion of the Japanese. They embrace it because they are a people who love cleanliness and because it is as relaxing as two or three martinis at the end of the day. In the winter it keeps them warm long after the bath, and in the summer, the air of the evening feels somehow less hot and oppressive after a long soak in 105-110 degree water. Visitors to hot springs usually bathe two and three times a day. In the isolated *onsen* town of Kawarayu near Ikao, retirees spend up to a month at a time in the baths during the idle, snowed-in months. One eighty-year old man in this town set a record by spending all of one winter in a bath.

The Ainu of Japan—that minority race of supposed Caucasoid origin—were reported in the early 1900's not to bathe at all, but now I suppose that they are nearly indistinguishable from the Japanese in such customs as bathing. (A number of famous men in recent history were also anti-bathing, including Ernest Hemingway, who rubbed himself with alcohol-soaked cloths and was probably as a consequence more hygienic than most confirmed bathers.)

American and Japanese attitudes toward the bath and its uses diverge largely at three points: One, of course, is the shower, that embodiment of the American dream of antiseptic efficiency. Granted, the Japanese say, it gets you clean, but ridding one's body of dirt, sweat, and germs is only part, although an essential part, of the cult of the bath. It does not relax the bather, they say, nor does it accomplish any of several other desiderata to be mentioned in this chapter.

We, in turn, question that anyone who baths in the same water with others can really get clean, even granting that each bather scrubs himself outside on the tile floor before entering the tub. This habit of having a number of persons bathe in the same water had its origin in the urgent necessity to conserve fuel, together with the fact that, given typical Japanese water-heating equipment, it would take entirely too long to heat (and to refill) a fresh tub for each member of the family. The Japanese try to enhance hygiene by filling their tubs to the brim and replenishing them so that there will be an overflow of water as each bather gets in, forcing such impurities as will float to leave the bath. Nevertheless, the water does get undeniably dirtier as the number using it increases, as can easily be witnessed by inspecting a public bath when it opens in the afternoon and then again when it closes in the late evening.

In addition to the shower, the Japanese also raise dubious eyebrows at our juxtaposition of the bathtub or shower and the toilet bowl. We consider that both are integral parts of the internal and external cleansing of the body and that it is only right (or at least not shocking) that they should stand side by side. The Japanese, on the other hand, see less essential connection between the two and feel, in fact, that the sight, odor, and (flushing) sound of a toilet bowl so close at hand can crush the aesthetic pleasure to be had from a leisurely, contemplative soaking. They would prefer that their baths be surrounded with flowers, moonlight, wind-bells, and nightingale song.

In a country short of most other resources, the Japanese

are blessed with an abundance of water. It surrounds them along a coast line 17,000 miles in length, and although they have few large lakes, their islands offer a finely-webbed pattern of clear, fast-running streams. They have plenty of well-timed rainfall, without which their wet-paddy rice would not grow. Their fondness for water manifests itself not only in their bathing but also in the largesse with which housewives and maids use water in homes.

And yet even here we find the paradox. Like all things, water must remain in its proper place to be used and enjoyed. Water in the bath is fine, but in improper places it is verboten. Leave your bath with a few cooling drops of neglected water on your back and shoulders and then notice the looks of shocked disapproval you earn.

Although the Japanese have produced such champion swimmers as Furuhashi, the Flying Fish of Fujiyama, they are far from being a nation of swimmers. Hordes jam the beaches near the cosmopolitan areas in late July and August, but the lures appear to be only incidentally aquatic.

Outside the major population centers, very few people enter the sea to swim. My wife's parents lived on a plateau overlooking the coast of Kagawa Prefecture in Shikoku and could see six magnificent beaches from their elevation. When I first visited them in the summer, I noted that these beaches were almost always deserted, with the occasional exception of someone gathering seaweed or shellfish. When I expressed amazement, a family council followed, at which it was decided that right-thinking men and women do not enter the sea for pleasure. (Nor were there any particular dangers, such as poisonous fish or sharks or treacherous currents, nearby. Just calm, clear water and clean, inviting sand.)

The third point—and perhaps the widest area of disagreement—about Japanese and American bathing practices concerns whether or not men and women, otherwise strangers to each other, should bathe together. Given their naturalistic acceptance of nudity (again, in its proper place), the Japanese custom of *konyoku* or mixed bathing should not be at all surprising. It has often been said that in Japan a naked person is seen but not really looked at. There are places and times in Japanese life in which it is necessary—or at least much the easier course—to appear wholly or partly unclothed before strangers (in unsegregated toilets and baths, aboard Pullmans, and in the pursuit of certain occupations). When this is the case, the Japanese have learned to accommodate others by not taking careful notice. They are taught that to ogle nudity is the epitome of barbarism. Obviously, they see what they see, but they reflexively glance elsewhere as a courtesy and in acknowledgment of the fact which they must all accept: that far too many Japanese are living in far too little space.

The Japanese are conditioned to expect this courtesy from other Japanese, but many of them have also come to expect intolerance, misunderstanding, shock, amusement, or possibly delight from us. To them, therefore, standing naked in front of a Japanese and standing naked in front of an American may be horses of two entirely different colors.

From the very beginning of our relationship with them, we have tended to give the Japanese a hard time about their unclothed moments, although it was really none of our blue-nosed business. Ensign McCauly, an American sailor who served under Perry on his first voyage to Japan, wrote in his diary, "I went into a bath house where girls of seventeen, old women, young women, old men were squatting on the stone floor, without rag enough to cover a thumbnail. . . . they invited us to join in and take a wash— but I was so disgusted with the whole breed, with their lewdness of manner and gesture, that I turned away with a hearty curse upon them."

Fortunately, one would have to go a long way to find a reaction like that among the men of today's navy.

In the Yokohama of 1862, mixed bathing in public baths was banned "by force of public opinion as expressed by the foreigners then resident there." Evidently not much heed was paid to the opinion of the vast majority, e.g., the Japanese, who just happened to own the country and who had not wanted the foreigners to come there to begin with.

Right thinking and good taste, however, must have prevailed throughout most of the remainder of the nation, for mixed bathing in the *onsen* continued to be permitted until shortly after the close of the Pacific War, when we again decided to try to play God with the morals of other people and urged the Japanese government to ban mixed bathing there as well as in the *sentō*, where it was already prohibited.

We met resistance but managed to set in motion forces that culminated before long in a new regulation and in enforcement of old ones. Early obedience to this law was only token and often took the form of a rope stretched across the middle of the pool-sized bath. Later, at police behest, some *onsen* operators erected board partitions in lieu of the ropes, but since these did not extend below the surface of the water, many of the more playful men merely ducked under it and came up on the other side, where they would soak, chin deep, with wash cloths over their heads. I cannot believe, however, that they did this with ogling as a primary motive; there was simply too much nudity around in Japan for a man to have to go that far out of his way to see it. Rather, it may have been a half-capricious gesture of defiance against an unrealistic law.

In time, more and more inns in cosmopolitan areas segregated their facilities, as did some in the more popular rural resort towns. When I heard occasional complaints from American tourists who had not been able to find the scenes of mixed bathing they had come so far to see, I assumed that the custom was dying away.

Shortly after that, I chanced to travel to the Daisetsuzan

National Park in Hokkaido and arrived one afternoon at a large inn where I had a reservation. As I was unpacking in my second-floor room, I heard from the ground floor below the sound of a great many young, exuberant voices. In a few minutes a maid came to lead me to the bath, as is the custom upon arrival, and as we approached that area on the ground floor, I realized that the tumult I had heard came from the bath, which the inn brochure had depicted as being of Olympic size.

I undressed in the men's dressing room and then opened the bathroom door onto an utterly charming scene.

About one hundred and fifty boys and girls were bathing together and apparently enjoying themselves immensely. They were all, I learned later, third-year students from a middle school in Sapporo, which meant that most of them should have been fourteen years old, give or take a year. They had come to the national park on a school-sponsored excursion together with a dozen male and female teachers. Nor were these teacher-chaperones shirking their duties. All of them were right there in the bath with their charges—and just as bare. Blase though I had thought myself to be, this experience was an eye-opener, though by no means an unpleasant one.

En route back to Tokyo, I stopped over in several more small towns, which were to serve as bases for my mountain climbing, and was pleased to learn that far from being moribund, mixed bathing was in fact thriving. Indeed, it seemed to have suffered no diminution at all. Subsequent inquiries confirmed that, once away from the depraved cities, Buddha is still in his heaven, and strangers of both sexes still bathe together. . . in some places.

I suppose that it is the surprise which we Americans evince that has conditioned many Japanese to become suddenly aware of their bareness before us. I remember hearing about a prime example of this reaction in what was surely one of the weirdest scenes ever enacted in Japan: A foreign photographer and his crew had gone to the remote Noto Peninsula on the Japan Sea Coast to film the Japanese women who dive, with bare bosoms, for pearls. But when these women saw that a disproportionately large segment of the attention of those foreigners was centered on their exposed breasts, they suddenly turned shy and self-conscious and refused to cooperate in the filming at all. The chief photographer tried several kinds of persuasion, all to no avail.

In despair, he discussed the problem with his crew, which included a comely American woman. At last they came up with the idea that the thing to do was to convince the people of the small village in which all the divers lived that bare breasts were nothing out of the ordinary in other countries, either. To this all the crew agreed. It just might work.

But how to bring about this conviction? Ahah! Several sets of male eyes fell on the lone female among them. What more effective way could there be than for this shapely American girl to stroll through the village streets herself, bare from the waist up?

I have no idea what, if any, methods were used in persuading that young American miss to comply, but stroll she did, in shoes, hose, skirt—and nothing else.

When her first Godiva-like jaunt failed to produce the desired results, she repeated her performance the following day. Again, no success. And the next day, with negative results.

I suspect that somewhere about here the male foreigners in the camera crew may have realized that the American girl's efforts were doomed to failure, but they wisely and watchfully kept her walking the streets of the village, building good will, as long as they could—until she at last rebelled. Then, just when they were packing to leave in defeat, they discovered that the gift of a skin diver's harpoon gun was all that was needed to win the hearts of the recalcitrant Japanese. After that they were permitted to make their movie and given full cooperation. . . and exposure.

Japan has 13,300 hot springs, of which 1,400 have mineral properties that are of medicinal value. A single spring is generally considered to be one localized underground source of hot water (they range from 80 to 226 degrees Fahrenheit), although several wells may tap the same source and two or three inns or a dozen or so homes may use the supply from one well. Around the more copious sources of supply, hot springs resorts, called *onsen-machi*, have grown up, especially where the circumambient scenery is noteworthy. The best-known *onsen-machi* include Beppu, Noboribetsu, Atami, Ikao, Miyanoshita, Kusatsu, Arima, Dogo, and Unzen.

Within each *onsen* inn, which can be identified by a mark that looks like an upside-down jelly fish and by the steam rising from a vent on its roof, the emphasis has always been on relaxation and submersion in the curative waters. Nowadays, however, the restless and increasingly affluent younger people are demanding more than these simple, old-fashioned pleasures. In response to this pressure from youth, the operators are adding bowling alleys, go-go parlors, pachinko or pinball games, pingpong tables, and other such exhilarating facilities.

The average *onsen* inn will have two or three *kazoku-buro* (family baths), in which three or four persons can bathe at the same time. The latter can be locked from inside, and some inns have taken to calling them, in their seductive literature, *romansu-buro* (romance baths), but I doubt that many Japanese couples would have any real reason to insist on such privacy. Again, we have the principle of everything in its proper place, which, in the case of sex, is in their room upstairs between *futon*. Besides, the surrounding tiles are too hard, and the Japanese have too much respect for bath water to stir it up in such a manner.

Many inns offer rooms with private baths. Where

possible, these are arranged so that one and sometimes two sides of the bathroom can be glassed-in. By building the inn on a slope, the various elevations are utilized so that the bathers are offered panoramic views of mountains or sea or both.

The list of the mineral properties of these many *onsen* and of the ailments they are reputed to cure is too long to quote, but most minerals and most complaints (including pregnancy) are wistfully included.

After my first year in Japan, I returned to the U.S. and spent a month in southern California near one of our American hot springs. Although I had visited many *onsen* in Japan during that first year, I had never been to one in my own country, and I was shocked and saddened by the difference. In the one in California, the atmosphere was suffused with the sad pungency of illness and age, of antiseptic decay, and of stoop-shouldered oldsters who talked endlessly about their ailments and doctors. I never entered the town without thinking of the laughter and ease, of the steamy air and cheerful amorality of Japan's *onsen*, where man and nature appeared to coexist on terms more amiable than elsewhere.

The foreign visitor to Japan would do well to find his own special *onsen* or Bali-hai or Shangri-la, if you prefer. I have mine: Three of them, one of which is so remote that the last leg of the journey is a 45-minute walk uphill. In this one, I find seclusion. In the second, I find scenery that is other-world in quality. In the third, I find extraordinary seafood and an old gentleman who raises bear-cubs and spins me tales of his boyhood.

The list from which you may choose is startling in its extremes of variety. For example, the Meitetsu Inuyama Hotel on Honshu has a bath that envelops its bathers in musical vibrations from loud-speakers installed underwater. The Kowakien Hotel in Miyanoshita boasts the largest single bath in Asia. The Dai Ichi Takimoto

Hotel in Noboribetsu, however, is the largest *onsen* establishment under one roof in the world: It has 23 separate baths, one of which is fifty yards long. In the middle of a broad, shallow river that flows through Shuzenji in the Izu Peninsula, there rises a spring that pours forth its hot water to blend with the chilly stream as both flow on. The municipality of Shuzenji has constructed a wooden walkway from the bank out to this *onsen*, which was discovered by a Buddhist priest in the ninth century. The dressing rooms, however, are on the river bank, so those who would take advantage of this free municipal bathtub must walk twenty yards in plain view of fishermen, loafers, tourists, and bright-eyed foreigners like myself—as naked as God or Buddha made them. Again, no Japanese appears to think anything of it.

Even more memorable, however, is an *onsen* inn on the Chita Peninsula, north of Nagoya, where man, not nature, made the physical arrangements. This inn has a mammoth communal bath, sixty yards long, in a room whose ceiling is three-stories high. When the men and women emerge from their separate dressing rooms, they must walk across an elevated path that is rather like a stage-passage through the audience, only higher. Because the male and female walkways are no more than fifteen yards apart, the men already in the bath are given a good upward view of all women—of necessity, naked—approaching and leaving their side of the bath, and vice versa. This particular bath is of recent construction, and it appears to be somewhat out of tune with the traditional Japanese attitude toward nakedness outlined earlier. One wonders if the efforts of the police to puritanize Japan, beginning in 1964, the year of the Olympics, may not already have aroused the Peeping Tom instinct in the breast of some Japanese men, with larger disasters to follow. (Peeping Toms are so rare in Japan that it takes most English-Japanese dictionaries several sentences to explain such an unheard-of creature.)

My most unforgettable *onsen* night was passed in the small resort town of Atagawa (meaning Warm River) on the eastern coast of the Izu Peninsula. Several American friends and I had gone hunting in the mountains that day and had returned to the inn at nightfall for boar sukiyaki. For some forgotten reason, I decided to bathe before my friends, so I asked my room maid to take me to the *rotenburo* or outdoor bath. Having been clambering up and down wet, slippery mountain paths most of the day, I was close to exhaustion and so took to the bath with me a bottle of Kirin beer, hoping that it would help me relax and recuperate.

It being the dinner hour, I was alone in the bath, once my maid had left. It was a night in November, which is perhaps the best month of the year in Japan, when the cool hand of autumn is felt but is softened by clear skies and a palpable sun. Above and to my right rose the now-dark shapes of the mountains, predominated by Mt. Amagi, that form the spine of the Izu Peninsula. To my left and below lay the Pacific, upon whose surface dancing lights had begun to appear. These were the lanterns that are hung from the prows of squid-fishing boats to attract those many-legged aquatics. The number of boats shortly doubled, then tripled, until soon there were more than a hundred of them bobbing about on the dark fluid surface.

The bath itself was designed to resemble a natural pool that one might stumble onto in the deep mountains, studded with large rocks and half-hidden by foliage. After four or five minutes in its hot water, the bather could stand up and then, but only then, find the chill night air a welcome relief.

Alone there in the relaxing water, with the sound of revelry from the inn faint enough to enhance, not diminish, the aura of anticipatory pleasure, I slowly felt myself becoming more and more an integral part of nature instead of a mere intruder. The mountains and the sea, the moon and the stars, the cool autumnal evening and the hot spring pool among the natural foliage—I felt that I was one with them, and I remained there for nearly an hour, unconscious of time and enthralled by an insight into what nature and the *onsen* may mean to the Japanese.

Sentō (written "money" and "hot water") is Japanese for public bath. Usually these are large low buildings with towering chimneys. The *sentō* open at three in the afternoon, which is when most mothers bring their babies to take advantage of the cleanest water, and close at eleven-thirty at night.

At the entrance, the bather removes his shoes and pays the fee to the cashier on duty at a lectern-like counter overlooking both the male and female sides of the bath. Inside he takes a basket, undresses, places his clothes in the basket, which he then leaves on a shelf. From this dressing room he steps down a few inches onto the tiled floor of the bath proper, a spacious room with a 10′ by 12′ pool on the far side and with water faucets placed low all along its walls. The pool will hold up to twenty bathers at one time, and there may be even more squatting on small wooden stools and scrubbing themselves (obligatory before entering the bath) near the faucets, from which they can draw hot and cold water to ladle over themselves from wooden pails with handles. One essential item of equipment is the *tenugui*, a small towel that the Japanese use as wash cloth, drying towel, and at times, fig leaf.(A wet cloth, incidentally, dries better than a dry one, for which there is a valid scientific explanation, although I have forgotten it.)

In addition to the *tenugui*, many Japanese will bring with them to the bath *hechima*, *nuka-bukuro*, and *karuishi*. *Hechima* is a dried gourd, rather like a sponge but without its absorbent power. *Nuka-bukuro* is like one of those bean-bags we used to make in kindergarten, only filled with bran instead of beans. Both the *hechima* and the *nuka-bukuro* can be used in lieu of wash cloths. *Karuishi* is a pumice stone, used, of course, to remove dead skin from the feet.

Some public baths—and *onsen* as well—employ *sansuke*, men who scrub the backs of bathers of both sexes. Unfortunately, there are no professional female *sansuke*, although a maid in an *onsen* inn may perform this service for the guest as one of her duties. The girls who work in Turkish baths (see below) might, however, be classed as *sansuke*, although they admittedly wash much more than just the back.

Among the families who have their own baths, the housewife must begin her preparations for evening ablutions about four in the afternoon. First, she drains out the water from the night before (which she may have used for various cleaning purposes during the day), washes out the wooden tub, and refills it, which takes fifteen or twenty minutes. Then she puts the cover on the bath and lights the fire. It will take twenty or thirty minutes to heat most baths, but some longer. (When we lived in Kamakura, it took forty minutes, my wife reminds me, to heat our bath, and this chore had to be done outside the house.) After that, the bath is ready, although the water will have to be replenished during the evening. (To maintain the temperature, a small fire is kept burning.)

While most baths are made of wood (cypress is best), there is another kind that resembles a large iron laundry pot and is called a *Goemon-buro*. The origin of the name is worth, I believe, at least this brief paragraph: Japan's Robin Hood was a robber named Goemon Ishikawa, who, when at last captured, was sentenced to be boiled to death in oil in such a pot, together with his very small son. (I suppose the authorities wanted to stamp out his breed forever.) With his son in his arms, Goemon was forced to stand in the pot, under which a fire was kindled. As the heat became increasingly painful, Goemon lifted his little boy over his head to keep him as far from the heat as possible, but when he felt himself begin to weaken, he suddenly plunged his son deep into the bubbling oil, to kill him as quickly as possible. Then, with his dead son in his arms, he stood up to shout defiance at his jeering enemies encircling him until he too succumbed to the pain and sank beneath the bubbling surface. Subsequently, cast-iron baths of that particular pot-like shape have been called *Goemon-buro* or Goemon baths in Japan, except in the Choshu district, where they may also be called *Chōshū-buro*.

Any guests in the home will be asked to bathe first. (If your Japanese host or hostess urges you to bathe, you needn't take umbrage. This is the height of courtesy, not an insult.) After the guests come the father and male children in order of age, then the distaff side of the family, followed lastly by any servants. A number of foreign authors who have written about the custom of the Japanese bath have made much over this order of precedence, but my own experience suggests that it is a custom as much honored in the breach as in the observance. During the three years, for example, that I lived with a middle-class Japanese family in Tokyo, the father usually bathed first, it is true, but after that it was a question of convenience and pending business as to who bathed next. One night the middle daughter might bathe after the father, because of a TV program that she wanted to see. The next night, the youngest boy might bathe before the oldest because he had just come back hot and sweaty from baseball practice. In fact, whenever one member of the family left the tub, the mother would go through the house calling out our names trying to find someone who wanted to take a bath at that particular time.

In that suburban home there were eight members of the family, including myself, and it always seemed to me that the bath was the center of familial attention from about four in the afternoon, when Mrs. M. began to drain and clean it, until eleven or eleven-thirty at night, when the final bather put the wooden lid back on the bath for the last time that day. The father usually had his bath right after dinner, at about seven, which took at least forty minutes. From then on it was a leisurely procession of bathers throughout the entire evening.

More affluent families sometimes have private baths that are large enough to hold most of their members at once. I have before me a color photograph showing a Mr. Tomogoro Nakanishi and his family at their evening ablutions. The grandfather and grandmother, their eldest son, and their grandson and granddaughter are in the tub together, while the eldest son's wife sits on the tiled floor beside the bath washing her second daughter. The tub is about six by six feet in size. Such intimacy is said to exert a strongly unifying effect on the Japanese family. (The family that bathes together stays together?)

In recent years, comparative studies of heart disease throughout the world have begun to focus increasing attention on the Japanese, who have the lowest incidence of that illness among the so-called civilized nations. Their preference for vegetable oils over animal fats is thought to be one explanation, but another of perhaps equivalent importance is their custom of a long, relaxing soak after work. (It is also an excellent substitute for cocktails, in that it stimulates the appetite without straining the liver or deadening the taste-buds.)

Can Humor Survive Translation?

Our second off-duty project at the Japanese language school involved trying to persuade our teachers, who were all first or second-generation Japanese, to teach us off-color jokes in that language. The first project, of course, had been the acquisition of certain essential items of vocabulary in the fields of sex, love, and vituperation.

In neither project did our efforts bear much palatable fruit. One teacher, a Mr. Nagai, told us a joke about *nigiri-meshi* or rice-balls which we thought was tolerably funny but which requires too much preparatory explanation in English to justify a translation here. Although I can't recall our being able to pry any other jokes out of our teachers, I was willing then to chalk this up to the faculty's concern about what kind of impression we would make when we first encountered "real" Japanese in Japan and to the fact that our level of ability in the language may not have been high enough for us to comprehend the more subtle humor.

When at last we reached Japan, my first experience with Japanese humor came one night when two of my classmates and myself were invited to the home of a Japanese family near Ohori Park in Fukuoka. After dinner, the three of us were seated on the tatami in their living room, drinking tea with the head of the family and his wife and three teen-aged daughters. During a brief lull in the conversation, our host lifted his right haunch slightly and complacently broke wind.

One of his daughters exclaimed, "*Mā, Otōsan!*" (My goodness, Father!), but she nevertheless joined her family in their laughter. They laughed so hard, in fact, that we started laughing with them, and it took everyone quite a while to recover their composure. After that, our visit was much less formal and more enjoyable.

Although I continued to watch for other examples of what would cause the Japanese to laugh, I did not, I must admit, make any special efforts in this direction, because we were already finding enough to laugh at in those days: mostly antics and incidents of our own contrivance. For example, we taught one of the new waiters in our mess-hall—a young man who knew almost no English—that it was exceedingly polite and very good form to enunciate the two words "You pig!" loudly and clearly whenever a guest from another unit asked for seconds during a meal.

At length I decided that if the Japanese wouldn't bring their humor to me, I'd bring ours to them and try to judge their capacity for humor by their reactions to ours.

One of my first experiments was to have a photographic enlargement of a famous Charles Addams cartoon framed and hung prominently in my room. This cartoon was the one that depicted a man skiing down a tree-dotted snow slope, the dual tracks made by his skis showing clearly behind him. At one point, however, the two ski-tracks diverge slightly, one passing a tree on the left side and the other passing the same tree on the right side. But below that tree, the skier and his skis are shown still to be all in one piece and functioning properly.

I suppose that several hundred Japanese saw—and stopped to study—that cartoon during the years it decorated the walls of my early homes in Japan. I never volunteered an explanation or asked for a reaction. My intent was only to observe. How many got the point, I cannot say. No one ever laughed. A few—less than ten—

asked me why I had hung the cartoon on the wall, but even they did not laugh when I tried to explain why I thought it was funny. At least, they did not *really* laugh. Some giggled rather nervously—and eyed me uneasily, while edging away.

In later years, I learned that this Addams cartoon was used extensively in psychiatric testing in the U.S., so I decided that perhaps it was not really a test of humorous capacity after all and took it down.

My classmates and I also tried from time to time to tell American jokes in Japanese. These never seemed to come off too well, but again I was willing to put most of the blame on our lack of perfection in the language. It was then that I decided that what I needed was an unsolicited American joke told by a Japanese.

In good time I found one in a magazine article written by a Japanese about his visit to the U.S. As an example of American humor, he related a joke—in Japanese, of course—that he had heard in Chicago:

A man was convicted of a crime and sent to prison. During his first week in prison, he noticed that several times every day his cell-mate walked to the front of their cell and shouted a number to the other prisoners in nearby cells. When they heard the number, the others chuckled or laughed. The new prisoner became quite curious, and when he could stand it no longer, he asked his cell-mate, "Say, buddy, what gives with all these numbers and those other cons laughing like that?"

"I guess I'd better tell you," said his cell-mate. "You see, we've been in stir so long that we know all of each other's jokes by heart. When it got so that it was too much trouble to tell the whole joke, we decided to assign each joke a number, so now all we have to do is shout out a number and the other guys remember that particular joke."

"Gotcha," said the new man. "Mind if I give it a try?"

"Go ahead."

"One hundred and sixteen!" the new man shouted down his cell-block.

Nothing happened.

"Two hundred and forty-six!" he yelled, trying again. Silence.

"Eighty-three!" the new man shouted once more.

Again, no reaction at all.

"Say, what am I doing wrong?" he asked his cell-mate.

"Well, some guys just don't know how to tell a joke," his cell-mate answered with a shrug.

Later the same day the cell-mate went to the front of their cell and yelled, "Three hundred and fifty!"

This brought the house down. The other prisoners whooped and hollered. They rolled on the floor. They laughed till they cried.

In exasperation, the new prisoner said, "I just don't understand it. They didn't crack a smile at my numbers but look how your number three hundred and fifty broke them up! I don't get it at all."

"Well, you see," the cell-mate explained, "they hadn't heard that one before."

I had no way of knowing how many readers of the Japanese magazine thought this story was funny, but I knew that it had impressed at least one Japanese—the author—and I knew that there was no doubt about the effectiveness of the Japanese wording, which I promptly committed to memory.

Over the next several years, at parties and dinners, I told that story many times, but I never got what I regarded as a gratifying response to it. A few titters, yes. An uneasy smile or two. But no genuine mirth.

Maybe, I thought, it's the wrong *kind* of joke. So I experimented with a series of other kinds, off-color, scatological, aggie, shaggy dog, sick, Polish, etc., but nothing changed my luck. Either I just couldn't tell a joke or the Japanese did not appreciate my style of humor. (I preferred to believe the latter.)

All this, however, should not be misconstrued to mean that the Japanese have no sense of humor. They do have one—and it is very well-developed, but it is one of those several things in Japan that do not export well.

R. H. Blyth, an English scholar who lived and taught in Japan for many years and who wrote a book about Japanese humor, said that he had found the Japanese to be the most humorous of all people. And he held that the best Japanese humor was contained in the *senryū*, those brief verses that attempt to isolate an essential point of human behavior and emotion, to debunk the pompous and self-deluding, and to poke fun at the backside of society. In his book, Blyth quotes three separate *senryū* that I find refreshing. (The translations are mine):

1)   *Waga shiri wa*
      Iwazu obi wo
Mijikagari

      Ignoring the size of her hips,
        She only grumbles
      That her sash is too short.

2)   *Kotsu-age ni*
      Naki naki
Kimba sagashite i

      She weeps and wails
        While she gathers the ashes of her
          loved one just cremated—
      But she does not forget to look for
        his gold teeth.

3)   Sewa-yatsure
Nete iru otto no
Hage ga mie

Dead tired from her house work
The wife notices her husband sleeping—
And the bald patch on his head.

Another authority on Japan, Basil Hall Chamberlain, said of Japanese humor, "It has no irony, no side-lights. It is more like what we may picture to ourselves in the practical joke, the loud guffaw, snatches of half-meaningless song, buffoonery, tomfoolery, high jinks of every sort, a very carnival of uproarious merriment. . . Often, no doubt, the expressions are coarse. . . spades are called spades."

Chamberlain refused, however, to translate examples of Japanese humor, pointing out that a "nation's fun is for home consumption only" and that "to undertake the explanation of any Japanese puns or other jokes would be a laborious business and cruel to the reader (and) still more cruel to the jokes."

In a series entitled *Yūmoa e no Shōtai* (Invitation to Humor), one Japanese newspaper says, in an article I have before me, that we foreigners are incapable of understanding Japanese humor. In illustration of its point, the newspaper mentions captions and photographs taken by LIFE photographer Carl Mydans at the time of the disastrous earthquake in Fukui, Japan.

Mydans had chanced to be in the city of Fukui when the earthquake struck and had taken some vivid shots while buildings and homes were still shaking and crashing to the ground. One of his pictures showed a number of women running half-dressed out of a bath-house, some smiling slightly. Another picture was of a dying carpenter just after he had jumped from the fifth floor of a building. He too was smiling.

I do not remember the English captions in LIFE myself but according to this Japanese newspaper, they suggested perplexity over the fact that the half-dressed, terrified women and the dying carpenter were smiling.

Then the newspaper goes on to explain that the women were smiling to cover their embarrassment and confusion at being unexpectedly seen in that condition by a stranger—and especially by a foreign stranger. The carpenter had forced himself to smile, the newspaper said, in apology for inadvertently letting his suffering be seen by a foreigner. He must have felt that it was bad manners to cause a stranger concern over his own suffering. With his weak smile, he was trying to say, "Don't worry about me. I'm all right. Don't let me detain you."

(Although I agree that most foreigners do not understand what is in back of the Japanese smile, this newspaper was wrong in equating an understanding of the Japanese smile with an appreciation of Japanese humor.)

I have seen Japanese delivery boys smile after tumbling off their bicycles and spilling six tiers of trays of noodle bowls, even though they knew that they would probably be docked a week's wages. I have seen men smile while being arrested for reckless driving. And I have seen them smile when telling me about the death of a member of their immediate family. These smiles are mystifying to foreigners, but in the first two cases, the Japanese were smiling to cover their embarrassment and chagrin. And in the third, their purpose was to shield an outsider from exposure to a sadness that is not his.

This smile can also be infuriating. I remember once, shortly after I first went to Japan, going to a photo-developing shop for the third time to pick up some pictures that should have been developed and printed five days before that.

Seward: "Good evening. Are my pictures ready?"

Clerk: "Mr. Seward, wasn't it? No, I'm sorry, they're not ready yet."

Seward: "That's what you told me the last time, but you promised that they'd be ready today."

Clerk, grinning: "I'm sorry."

Seward, burning: "What's so funny?"

Clerk, grin broadening: "There's nothing funny."

Seward: "Don't tell me there's nothing funny! You're smiling, aren't you?"

Clerk, on the point of open laughter: "I'm sorry, but your pictures aren't ready yet."

Exit Seward, puzzled and beaten. Curtain.

What I did not understand then was that he smiled because he instinctively felt that trouble was in the offing. He must have had difficulties with other Americans before on that same score. He was wrong, of course, in not having the pictures ready on the date promised, but I was wrong in thinking that he saw any humor in the situation. Doubtless he was merely uneasy at the prospect of having another American explode in anger in his shop and was smiling instinctively as the first thing to do in such a situation.

Obviously the Japanese smile when they are happy or pleased, just as they smile and laugh when they are amused, but whenever a foreigner sees a Japanese smile at *other* times, he should regard that smile as a signal to veer off, to probe no deeper. That smile may be covering sorrow or anger or momentary perplexity at what should be done in difficult circumstances. In any case, this smiling Japanese does not want you to push any further into the matter. He is giving you a clear signal, as politely as he knows how, that you should drop the present topic of conversation or course of action. You, in turn, should return the smile as a signal that you comprehend—and that you will comply.

Japanese humor in its purest form is to be found today in the *rakugo* and *manzai* performed on the stages of small halls and, to a lesser extent, on television. In the case of the former, a man sits on the tatami and tells a story, often taking the roles of two or three players. Among these *rakugo* artists are wonderfully competent actors who can perform miracles of characterization and narration by the flip of a fan or the elevation of an eyebrow or a subtle change in vocal timbre. In the case of the *manzai*, two persons sit or stand on the stage to act out a humorous incident or tell a series of loosely-connected funny stories. More slap-stick enters into this latter form.

To try to show a foreign reader what is funny in these performances involves not merely translation but also often complicated linguistic explanation, for many of them—most, perhaps—depend on plays on words for their humor. Consider this excerpt from a typical stage dialogue:

First man: "*Oi, ore wa tobei suru nda yo!*" (Hey, I'm going to America!)

Second man: "*Ē?*" (Huh?)

First: "*Tobei suru ndatte.*" (I said I'm going to America.)

Second: "*Nani?*" (What?)

First: "*Tobei-tte! Tobei!*" (Going to America, I said! Going to America!)

Second: "*Doko made?*" (How far?)

(Laughter and applause.)

The point is that *tobei* is a noun meaning to go to America. (The addition of *suru* makes it a verb.) But *tobu* is the infinitive form of the verb meaning to jump, and *tobe* is its imperative form, meaning "Jump!" The straight man above is mistaking *tobei* (going to America) for *tobe!* (Jump!). Explaining it like this takes the life out of it, but it is tolerably funny if it is fast-paced and well done on the stage or T.V.

Despite our early difficulties in getting our language school teachers to tell us jokes in Japanese, the Japanese do have such, although they don't exchange them nearly as much as we Americans do. (One reason for this is that joke-telling, to the Japanese, is an activity only for equals. For an inferior to tell a superior a joke would be presumptuous; for a superior to tell one to an inferior would be inviting unwanted intimacy. And in Japan, very few people are equals.) Here is an example (off-color, fortunately, as most of them are):

Three nuns were walking down a country road when they happened to see a stud horse about to mount a mare, with his weapon elongated and in full view. At first, the nuns pretended that they didn't notice what was happening, but then all three began to giggle and finally one of them suggested, "Let's play a game: Each one of us will think of a name for that *thing* and then explain why she chose to call it that."

"All right," the other two agreed. "You go first, Sister."

"I'll call it o-sake," the first nun said, "because no matter whether you take it at night or during the day, it makes your heart rejoice."

"I'll call it *ume-boshi,*" the second nun said, referring to the pickled plums that the Japanese inexplicably regard as great delicacies, "because whenever I think of it, it makes my mouth water."

"I'll call it *hana-kenuki,*" the third nun said, referring to the tweezers that are made especially for plucking hairs from the nose.

"Why *hana-kenuki,* Sister?" asked the other two nuns, puzzled.

"Because," she explained, "everytime you pull it out, a few tears come out, too!"

I should perhaps explain that in the world of Japanese jokery, nuns and priests are favorite subjects who are forever engaged in riotous living and sexual hanky-panky. Once when I was engaged in a research project in Japanese history, I came across the word *bikuni,* with which I was not familiar and which I finally learned meant "nun-prostitute." My curiosity aroused, I investigated further and discovered that not only had there been such creatures but that they had existed in sufficient numbers to justify the coining of a special word to describe them. Evidently they were taken into religious orders as nuns and were then used not only to provide the priests with sexual release but also sent out into the countryside from time to time to earn "alms" for the temple with their bodies.

Here is another example:

A new serving girl is hired to work at a temple. After she has been there several days, the head priest crawls into her dark room late one night.

"Who is it?" she asks, startled. Then, "Oh, it's you, master."

"Shhh," the priest cautions her. "Lower your voice."

Then he crawls in between her *futon* and has his will of her.

Afterwards, she offers him several sheets of soft, thin paper, but he declines them and uses his loin-cloth instead.

"Why don't you use this paper, master?" the girl asks.

"Being a priest, I don't dare," he explains. "It would be sacrilegious for me to use *kami* that way."

The point of this joke is that the word *kami* means both paper and god.

Although it is unintentional, there is another kind of humor to be found in Japan—in English signs, menus, labels, announcements, etc. written by Japanese.

One of my first encounters with this kind of humor came shortly before the first Christmas after the war when I strolled from the Yuraku Officers' Billet in Tokyo over to the Ginza to do some Christmas shopping for relatives and friends at home. I was accompanied by Commander Lou Spaeth of the U.S. Navy, an old friend who later was the source of some of the "Translation Sensations" I will mention herein.

Reaching the Ginza, Lou and I found a small crowd of foreigners gathered outside one of the department stores— I believe it was the Matsuzakaya—and staring up at a mammoth banner.

The banner read, "Christmas Paint Your Harts."

Puzzlement was written large on the faces of the foreigners. We overheard one sergeant say to the corporal beside him, "Now what the devil do you suppose that means?"

We never were sure about the meaning ourselves, but the banner clung to my memory as the opening curtain of a long and memorable experience with Fractured English in Japan. The many other examples I encountered over the years were delightful, refreshing, and often hilarious. They were instructive in that they showed a people striving mightily to communicate with a horde of foreigners suddenly in their midst, efforts that even when laughable, at least deserved top grades for effort. (Few of *us* spent much time learning Japanese.) And with the passage of time I found that some of these instances of broken English had a piquant charm about them that somehow communicated the author's meaning even better than standard correct English might have.

An example of this latter variety was a sign in front of the Nikko Botanical Gardens that read, "No Botanizing, drinking, or uproaring, etc. in the garden." That left no doubt about what they meant . . . *and* made a lasting impression.

The language of signs (or "Sign Langwich," as one Japanese sign-painter advertised his product) offered a most fruitful field, with little gems like these:

"Fondle dogs" (from a pet shop in Osaka)

"First-class lady toilet" (aboard a ship called the *Himeyuri-maru*)

"We wash you" (from a car-wash in Kawasaki)

"Guaranteed pure gold fish" (from a goldfish peddler's cart)

"We sell curious art goods" (from a brassware shop in Fukuoka)

"Specialist for the Decease of Children" (from an Osaka pediatrician's office)

"Extract of fowl" (from an egg store)

One sign at the airport in Haneda seemed to uncannily predict the future of airline baggage services all over the world: "We Take Your Bags and Send Them in All Directions."

Hotels were also good hunting grounds for the happy Fractured English Hunter:

"Use this elevator. Fright Elevator in repair." (in the Shiba Hotel in Tokyo)

"The elevator is fixed for the next day. During that time we regret you will be unbearable." (in a Niigata hotel)

"Our hotel serves ten in a bag—like Mother." (in a hotel near the docks in Kobe)

"Rooms are changing their boys and girls." (notice left in each room in an engineers' billet in Yokohama, presumably by the room-boy)

"Room-boy is a present." (from a card attached to a small gift left in my room by the room-boy in Tokyo's Dai Ichi Hotel)

Consider also the following names of products: Creap (a powdered coffee cream), Puddy (a prepared pudding mix), Calpis (a soft drink that I somehow associate with bovine urine), Peculiar Cold Cream, Kitchy Miso Soup (a powdered soup base), and the Cedric car (imagine a Detroit automobile manufacturer naming one of its models Tom or Erskine or Sammy).

Although I never found proof of my suspicions, I used to like to darkly imagine that somewhere down in the dim, dank cellars under the national police forces headquarters in Tokyo, there dwelt a musty gnome of a man with tousled hair and a fanatic glint in his eyes. Ensconced among his trusty lexicons, he was charged with the English translation of all the traffic signs that were to be erected along the roads and streets of his country. It was his little empire ("Mine! All mine!"), and his translations were never to be questioned. His word was god-like and final, and he never deigned to verify his translations with native speakers of English for accuracy.

Among his masterpieces were:

"Cars will not have intercourse on this bridge." (from a bridge near Fukuoka)

"Let's Reduce Noise by Ourselves." (In one particular year, there were hundreds of these signs erected all along the byways of Japan.)

"Vertical parking only." (a sign on the street in front of the old Teito Hotel in Tokyo)

"Slow men working!" (a sign near a stretch of road being re-paved in Shinjuku)

"Quietly!" (This sign was also erected by the hundreds or even thousands throughout the country. The Japanese equivalent was "*Shizuka ni*," which can, of course, be rendered as "Quietly!" but which in this instance carries with it the strong connotation of "Be calm, slow down, take care.")

"Have many accidents here!" (a sign at the Roppongi intersection in Tokyo)

The last of the above nearly caused an international incident when I first sighted it. It must have been the devil that made me do it, but I reported to a nearby police box and explained that, being a law-abiding sort of fellow, I insisted on obeying traffic signs to the precise letter and therefore wanted to know just where I should have the accidents mentioned in the sign and how many persons I should arrrange to have injured in them.

A surly lot, the Roppongi police could see little if any

humor in this and made unwarranted threats against my future freedom of movement.

Akin to this traffic-sign gnome in the police cellars, there was also, I am confident, an absolute linguistic genius squirreled away backstage in that marvellous hall of pleasure: the Nichigeki Theater. He was the man who, for many years, made up the titles (all in flawless English) for the song and dance productions shown in the Nichigeki Music Hall. It greatly behooves some ardent young researcher of good will to go through the Nichigeki ads in the old newspaper files and record for future enlightenment the magnificent titles this genius confected. I remember three, that were Jim Dandies:

"Titillate Me Purple in the Tulip Time"

"Shag and Shimmy at the Shine-town Shindig"

"Three Dervishes at a Whippenpoof Whingding"

Just across the alley from the Nichigeki stood the Asahi Bldg., where labored mightily the editors of the *Asahi Evening News*. One of these fellows concocted the idea of a contest in which this English-language newspaper would offer ¥1,000 for examples of weird Japanized English. This contest produced some spanking good ones, including, I recall, a photograph of a medicine bottle, the label of which read: "Adults: Take three tablets a day until passing away."

But finally the great, grey eminence of the *Asahi* got caught in its own toils the day they ran this headline: "Solution to Laotian Crisis Remains Unsolved."

Lest I be accused of poking fun only at the Japanese, I hasten to point out that during those same years we Westerners in Japan must have been—despite our lower level of linguistic activity—guilty of monumental bloopers that had even the normally restrained and polite Japanese rolling in the aisles. Sadly, one has to understand Japanese to appreciate these offenses against proper language use, but I may give a hint of their magnitude by pointing out two words similar in sound but quite different in meaning: *komon* means advisor, but *kōmon* means anal exit, the only difference being the long or short sound of the first 'o' in the two words. I had an American acquaintance who once introduced himself at a conference of Japanese businessmen with the Japanese equivalent of the sentence: "I am Mr. Sasakawa's advisor." At least, that is what he *intended* to say—but he inadvertently used the long 'o' instead of the short 'o.' He broke up the conference.

In a proud window sign, a department store in Niigata had this to say about one of its items of merchandise: "Our nylons cost more than common but will find best for long run."

In general, not only department stores but also tailors, dressmakers, and fashion stores were quite magnanimous with their Fractured English creations:

"New and Old Clothes Fix Civilized Style." (from a Nihombashi tailor shop)

"We Make Fur Out of Your Skin." (from a fashionable fur shop on the Namiki-dori in Tokyo)

"Stateside Stile" (from a Ueno dressmaker's store)

"Ladies Have Fits Upstairs." (that old classic from a dressmaker's establishment near the Daibutsu statue in Kamakura)

"Dresses for Ladies and Gentlemen" (chiselled in the marble facade above a Ginza clothing store)

"European Monkey Jacket Make for Japanese" (example quoted in a book by B. H. Chamberlain)

Many jewels were mined in bars (where I found "Old American Whiskey—Established 1492" and "Old Airship Whisky—Since Early 1800's") and in restaurants' menus, such as:

"Sardine Sand"	"Humbug Steak"
"Cuban Livers"	"Rogue Fart Cheese"
"Beef Strong Nuff"	"Prown and Poison Au Gratin"

One Shinjuku bar yielded, in its toilet, the carefully-lettered sign: "To stop drip, turn cock to right."

The famous Deer Park in Nara warned its visitors to "Beware of Bucks with Long Horns." On the window of a photographer's studio was painted "Photographer Executed," and in the same neighborhood stood a sundries store with the sign, "Sun Light Soap—Lever Brothels, Ltd."

For a while I puzzled over an English-language map of Tokyo showing a location near Tokyo Bay with the description, "Dirty Water Punishment Place." Checking the original Japanese, I learned it was a Sewage Disposal Plant, but the linguistic complications leading from there to "Dirty Water Punishment Place" are too lengthy and tortuous to set down here.

Another puzzling sign was found in a suburban Tokyo shop window, with no other indication as to the nature of the store or what product or service it wanted to sell. I never did enter to find out; I think I was uneasy about what I might be told. The sign, in its entirety, read:

"Come in and have your thing engraved."

In *Things Japanese*, author B. H. Chamberlain mentioned a booklet distributed to Japanese policemen entitled, "*The Practical Use of* (English) *Conversation for Police Authorities*," which is divided into such chapters as "Cordinal Number," "Official Tittle," and "Ports of the Body."

Under "Misseranious Subjects" is offered an imagined conversation between a Japanese policeman and a British sailor:

Policeman: "What countryman are you?"

Sailor: "I am sailor belonged to the Golden Eagle, the British man-of-war."

Policeman: "Why do you strike this *jinrikisha* man?"

Sailor: "He told me impolitely."

Policeman: "What does he told you impolitely?"

Sailor: "He insulted me saing loudly 'the Sailor, the Sailor' when I am passing here."

Policeman: "Do you striking this man for that?"

Sailor: "Yes."

Policeman: "But do not strike him for it is forbidded."

Sailor: "I strike him no more."

Toward the end of this booklet, the author himself appears to have his own private doubts about what he has wrought, for he injects a conversation between two policemen that ends on this note:

First policeman: "You speak English very well."

Second policeman: "You jest."

During WW II, the prisoner of war camp at Omuta produced a splendid specimen of Fractured English in this announcement to its POW's:

(a) It is forbid to kill the commandmant (Penalty: Kill-ed to death and the life imprison).

(b) It shall be prevent to damage the commandmant (Penalty: Life imprison and punish).

(c) It shall be forbid to plot to kill the commandmant (Penalty: Shoot-ted to death and the life imprison).

(d) It shall be forbid to steal of Japanese Army (Penalty: Heavy punish, life not assured).

(e) All prisoner shall take care of their health.

But quite possibly the one classic instance of Fractured English in Japan that must tower over all competition was seen when Douglas MacArthur was still enthroned in Tokyo and was being promoted as a possible candidate in the pending U.S. presidential election. A group of ardent Japanese supporters of the already aging general arranged to have a gigantic banner hoisted high over the busy Hibiya intersection in downtown Tokyo, just where MacArthur could see it when he emerged from his office in the Dai Ichi Building. Bearing in mind that the Japanese tend to confuse the 'r' and the 'l' in English, try to visualize these six-foot high letters emblazoned on the banner:

"WE PRAY FOR MACARTHUR'S ERECTION!"

Colorful Ways of Departing This World

During the Sengoku Era in Japanese history, the commander of one of Lord Mori's castles, Muneharu Shimizu, was ordered to commit hara-kiri: suicide by disembowelment.

On the evening of the hara-kiri ceremony, a loyal vassal of Shimizu's—a man named Shirai—sent a message to his master begging that he deign to come to Shirai's room. Although understandably preoccupied with thoughts and preparations for his departure from this world, which was to take place in less than an hour, Shimizu took the time to go to his favorite vassal's quarters in a far corner of the castle. When Shimizu got there, Shirai was sitting with his legs crossed on the tatami matting. Humbly he asked his master to sit down beside him, whereupon he began to tell Shimizu he should not fear death, he should approach it with courage and equanimity, and self-disembowelment was not, after all, such a fearful demise.

Shirai coughed once and swayed slightly. Then he opened his robe.

"You see, sire," he said, revealing the bloody slash across his abdomen, "I committed hara-kiri myself as soon as I was sure you were coming. I wanted to show you it is not so difficult. . ."

Overcome with gratitude, Shimizu rose to his feet beside his faithful vassal and unsheathed his long sword. With tears in his eyes, he raised his blade and with it cut off Shirai's head, thereby performing the act of *kaishaku* and

69

according his old friend high honor.

After a few minutes of silent grief, he cleaned his sword and then walked back to meet his own end—with renewed courage.

A similar but little-known incident took place in 1944 in Cowra, Australia, when the Japanese inmates of a prisoner-of-war camp broke out of captivity and fled into the Australian countryside one night in August. When the Australian guards entered the prisoners' barracks after the break, they found the bodies of eleven Japanese hanging from roof-beams. Interrogation of prisoners recaptured later revealed those eleven men had been the instigators of the escape and they had hanged themselves in front of all the other prisoners to demonstrate their own willingness to die and to give their comrades courage.

These two instances should suggest that the Japanese institution of suicide is a remarkable, if not unique, phenomenon in mankind's annals of reasons for and methods of self-destruction.

Although Westerners perhaps think of hara-kiri first in connection with Japanese suicides, the earliest recorded cases in Japan were accomplished by hanging and self-incendiarization, the usual manner of the latter being for the victim to set fire to his own home with himself inside.

Yoshiteru Murakami, a warrior of Japan's feudal days, managed to combine both self-incendiarization and hara-kiri in his own dramatic demise, when he and his master, Prince Morinaga, were trapped in a house by their enemies. Wanting to distract the foe so his master could escape, Murakami climbed to the roof with a torch in his hand. With it, he set fire to the thatch, which blazed up brightly while Murakami yelled taunts to the enemy samurai below in the garden.

"Dogs!" Murakami shouted, "I am Prince Morinaga. Watch! I'll show you cowards how a true warrior dies."

In the light of the leaping flames from the thatched roof,

Murakami glanced back and saw the dim form of Prince Morinaga disappear over the garden wall at the back side of the house. Reassured, he turned back to the now intently watching foe clustered on the ground below him.

Silently he shed his outer robe and withdrew his dagger. Steeling himself, he made a long, deep slash across his abdomen, just below the navel. Despite the excruciating pain and the now-blinding heat, he kept his body straight and his face impassive. As his intestines came tumbling out through the cut, he seized a handful with his left hand and cut them loose with the dagger in his right.

Tossing the dagger aside, he threw the ropy intestines down into the faces of his startled enemies. Then with one final effort he unsheathed his long sword, inserted the point in his mouth, and fell forward on it and into the flaming thatch.

This was one of the first recorded instances of hara-kiri or seppuku (both mean stomach-cutting) in Japanese history and took place long before it had become a formalized ceremony, encumbered with almost as many traditions and rules as the coronation of a monarch.

Sen-no-Rikyu, one of a long line of justly celebrated tea-ceremony masters, was another who cut part of his own intestines free from his body. He had been ordered to commit seppuku by Hideyoshi, the de facto ruler of Japan at the time, for reasons Sen-no-Rikyu thought were unjust. Although he followed Hideyoshi's orders, he made his indignation known by cutting loose a portion of his own intestines, piling them in coils on a tray, and insisting, with his dying breath, that they be delivered to Hideyoshi.

Seppuku became popular among the Japanese as a means of ending one's life partly because the stomach was regarded as the seat of all emotions, the abode of the soul. Their language has many expressions that support this: *Hara ga tatsu* (the stomach stands up) means to get angry. *Hara-guroi hito* (a man with a black stomach) means a sly, cunning man. *Hara wo kimeru* (to decide the stomach) is the equivalent of to make up one's mind. *Kare no hara ga yomenai* (I cannot read his stomach) is similar to saying I cannot understand what's in his mind.

One little-understood aspect of formalized seppuku is that the stomach-cut alone was usually not fatal. This incision was made from left to right just below the navel but was not deep. The above-quoted cases in which the intestines poured out through the wound were exceptional and took place before seppuku became a ritualized method of punishment. Some men, in fact, barely scratched themselves with the tips of their daggers. It was after this cut had been made that the kneeling man signalled, by nodding his head or raising a finger, for his assistant, who was waiting poised to his left rear, to chop off his head. The role of this assistant also became formalized and required great skill. Some were able to lop off a head and leave it hanging from the trunk of the body by only a shred of skin. To cut the head off entirely was considered poor form, since it was liable to roll around and perhaps even bespatter distinguished witnesses with blood.

Nowadays, however, seppuku—together with Bushido, the Code of the Samurai—has fallen into disuse. Although there have been a few subsequent cases, the last significant number took place at the end of the Pacific War. (Admiral Onishi—a primary force in the development and use of the Special Attack or Kamikaze Corps, which was another colorful facet of Japanese suicides—was among those who disembowelled themselves soon after learning of Japan's decision to surrender. Onishi made the stomach-cut before dawn on August 16, 1945, and then, having no assistant, tried to bring on death by cutting his own throat. Neither cut, however, was deep enough, so he lingered on in pain until his final breath at six o'clock that evening, having refused all offers to either hasten or hinder his departure.)

While nothing has taken the place of seppuku, which was

both a ceremony and a punishment ordered by the authorities or a feudal lord, other forms of Japanese suicide are, of course, still with us, rich in variety and significant in number.

One popular fashion of exit-making is called *ressha-ōjō*: throwing oneself in front of a train. Sometimes a pair of unhappy lovers will tie themselves together with the girl's sash and then fall onto the tracks. In another common method of double-suicide (which the Japanese call *shinjū*, meaning to reveal the heart), the star-crossed lovers, again bound to each other, leap from a high cliff into the sea or a river.

In those instances of *shinjū* in which the lovers do not bind themselves together, the male—displaying that eminent sensibility for which the Japanese man is famed—often follows the Western custom of ladies first.

This gives the man a breathing spell and allows him time to consider his options. The sight of his true love lifeless toward the bottom of the crater of Mt. Aso or being whirled about by the frothing water among the boulders beneath Kegon waterfall may give him pause for serious thought.

Sometimes he jumps anyway. At other times he calls it a day and heads for home, either deciding to forget the whole thing or to plan it for another day. Famous author Osamu Dazai (*No Longer Human*) tried with four women (three of whom died) before he at last succeeded with a fifth.

Japanese authors, in fact, seem to be particularly prone to the lure of self-destruction. Several of the notables who have done themselves in include Tokoku Kitamura, Takeo Arishima, Ryunosuke Akutagawa (of the prestigious Akutagawa Award fame), Bizan Kawakai, Yasunari Kawabata (winner of the Nobel Prize for Literature, who wrote, "There is no art superior to death"), and, of course, Yukio Mishima.

I chanced to be with Hiroshi Funasaka, the man who

gave Mishima the sword with which he was decapitated, on that fine fall day in 1970 when Mishima, an apparent homosexualist and frustrated war-lover, stood on the balcony of the Eastern Army headquarters of Japan's Self-Defense Forces and harangued the soldiers assembled below him to revolt and overthrow the government and return the Emperor and Japan to their rightful places in the Heavens.

The soldiery merely laughed and jeered.

Disappointed (or had Mishima fully anticipated this reaction?), the renowned author stepped back inside, where several members of the Shield Society, a quasi-military group Mishima had formed and trained, waited for him.

Baring his abdomen, he made the obligatory horizontal cut of the suicide ritual that had fascinated him so long, then signalled to his *kaishaku* to cut off his head.

In appreciation for having taught his son the rudiments of kendo, my friend Hiroshi Funasaka had given Mishima an old sword so famous in Japanse history that, like the Excalibur of King Arthur, it had a name of its own: *Seki-no-Magoroku*. But because the *kaishaku* had had no experience in lopping off human heads, he botched the job. It took him three cuts to completely separate Mishima into two pieces, badly knicking the blade in the process.

We were in Funasaka's office in the Taiseido, the book store he owns in Shibuya in Tokyo, when his secretary burst into the room with the news.

Funasaka blanched. He tried to speak but could not. Knowing there was nothing I could do to ease his dismay, I cancelled our luncheon appointment and left quietly.

Committing suicide to draw attention to oneself or to one's dilemma is by no means limited to Japan, but this reason deserves special emphasis there and helps to explain the often bizarre ways by which the Japanese voluntarily depart this life.

Jumping from the top of department stores to sidewalks below is one such method that should surely be classed as a strong bid for attention, especially when we consider that the majority take place during rush-hours.

At noon of one spring day in 1948, I was looking out from the window of my office in Osaka and happened to see a man jump from the top of a department store across the canal from my building. He landed on top of three young office girls, who had been walking along hand-in-hand enjoying the sunshine, killing one and injuring the other two. I had first caught sight of him when he climbed over the guard wire and noticed that he had placed a black box on the ledge beside him before taking his final leap.

The deaths and injuries had, of course, drawn quite a crowd, but the people on the street could not see the black box eight stories above them, so I left my office, crossed the canal by a nearby bridge, and went up to discover that the box was a portable record-player and that the record to whose strains the young man had dived to his death was *Mood Indigo*.

Throwing oneself into the pit of a volcano is another familiar method of self-disposal, in which perhaps tidiness is a factor, since there really is no problem of disposal of the corpse, it being swallowed up by molten lava. For those so inclined, the active volcanoes of Mihara (on Oshima) and Aso (in Kyushu) are highly regarded.

Other places that have become famous as suicide sites are Nishikigaura, a seaside cliff near Atami from which lovers leap, and Kegon-no-taki, a waterfall near Nikko into whose tumultuous basin singles and couples alike plunge with ultimate abandon.

In a recent year the mistress of the president of a Tokyo company took a bath, killed herself, and took revenge on her patron and his wife all at the same time. The company president had decided to break off the liaison with his mistress and to spend more time with his wife (surely a newsworthy item in itself in Japan), but the extra-legal bed-mate demanded more consolation money than he was willing to give. With things at this impasse, he moved his possessions out of his mistress's apartment. Before he did, however, she was able to lay her hands on the key to his legal domicile long enough to have a duplicate made.

A week or so later, the man took his wife out for dinner one evening (another newsworthy happening), and the ex-mistress, who had been spying on their home for several nights, used her duplicate key to gain entry. Once inside, she drew a hot tub, found a razor, and undressed. After a leisurely bath, she settled herself comfortably in the steamy water and cut both her wrists.

I suspect that she may have died gleefully imagining the look on the face of her ex-lover's wife upon finding a strange woman taking a blood-bath in her bathtub—and the noisy scuffle that was sure to follow.

The socio-cultural reasons for most Japanese suicides are such conditions as shallowness of religious belief, stress arising from continuing social changes, lack of conjugal communication, the concept that death will atone for sins committed during one's life, financial problems and the lack of adequate social welfare, the traditional belief that death is pure and beautiful, and a tendency to place excessive reliance on the help and good will of family and friends instead of relying on one's own resources.

Against this background, we find the Japanese departing prematurely for the *takai* (other world) for such reasons as failing a school exam, losing a contest or game, and even a desire to call the attention of a foreign country to Japan's problems. And up until the end of the war in 1945, men were known to kill themselves for very slight and even unintentional acts of discourtesy to the Emperor and the Imperial Family, e.g., momentarily holding the Emperor's photograph upside down or allowing the Imperial train to depart two minutes late.

These and other reasons are often so seemingly un-important that the foreign observer is led to the possible explanation that the Japanese simply do not hold life, theirs or anyone else's, as dear as we do. Or that they do not regard death as the awful, ultimate tragedy that we believe it to be.

I, for one, place some credence in the latter explanation. My own observance of death in Japan has suggested to me that many Japanese continue to feel the immediate—almost physical, even if unseen—presence of loved ones who have died in the not-distant past. These souls or spirits apparently hover in and around the home instead of going away to some Western concept of heaven a million light-years off in space. With the passage of time, these spirits supposedly wander hither and yon on increasingly distant journeys, but they seem to do this gradually to accustom the living to their absence—and to return unfailingly at seasons like *O-Bon* and anniversaries of their deaths for visits.

Although Japanese students lead world studentry in suicides, the statistics covering all other segments of the population do not, surprisingly, support the notion that the Japanese people in general hold the record for the highest incidence of self-induced deaths.

The figures vary with the year, of course, but in a recent year West Berlin stood tall atop this heap, with Romania next. Ahead of Japan came Austria, West Germany, Denmark, Sweden, *inter alia*. That of the U.S. was low, but even lower ranked Italy and Ireland. And in Egypt, suicide was virtually unheard-of, their figure being only one one-hundredth of what it was in the U.S.

The most tragic aspect of suicide in Japan is that it all too often is an activity of youth: students who have failed to pass their college entrance exams for the second or third time, lovers who have been denied parental permission to marry, young widows who are having difficulty raising their children, and men, still under thirty, who die in apology for the sins or debts of their fathers. (In contrast, we find high rates of suicide in the U.S. among doctors, older divorced men, top executives, artists, and—significantly—psychiatrists.)

But whatever the age or reason, suicide in Japan stands far apart from suicide in the Western world because of prevailing attitudes toward it. Although our Bible (in which seven suicides are listed) does not specifically forbid the taking of one's own life, both the church and state have long brought moral and legal force to bear against it. (In the Middle Ages in Europe, everything belonging to a person who committed self-murder was taken away, his body was dragged through the streets and exhibited, and he was buried at a crossroads after a stake had been pounded into his heart.)

But in Japan as well as in much of Asia, suicide—for reasons of sacrifice or renunciation or expiation—has usually been regarded as admirable and even worthy of adulation.

In the Takanawa district in Tokyo, there is a small temple called the Sengakuji. Every year a multitude of people visit the cemetery in the temple grounds to pay their respects to the memory of the Forty-Seven Ronin and their master, who are buried there.

What these forty-seven masterless samurai did is so well-known that six kabuki plays and other stories without number have been written about their loyalty and courage. One of these kabuki plays—*Kanadehon Chūshingura*, pen-ned in 1748, is still performed yearly, from 14 December till year's end, with no sign of diminution of audience interest.

Had it been fiction, the story might not have been believed, at least not in the Western world.

In 1701, Naganori Asano was Lord of Ako, a town and district between Himeji and Okayama. His deadly enemy was a man named Yoshinaka Kira, protocol advisor to the Shogun. With insidious intent, Kira insulted Asano, who was not too conversant with the niceties of court protocol, in one of the passage-ways of the Shogun's palace. Enraged, Asano drew his sword and slashed at Kira.

Unsheathing one's sword in the hallowed interior of the Shogun's residence violated the rules of decorum, as Kira well knew, and so as a punishment the Shogun ordered Asano to commit ritual seppuku.

Asano's vassals did not question the punishment meted out to their master but believed that Kira too should have been ordered to commit seppuku, as a participant in the unseemly quarrel. Fifty-eight of them plotted revenge.

Knowing, however, that this would be expected of them, they went through the motions of disbanding and wandered off, as ronin or masterless samurai, in pursuit of dissolution and debauchery. Their leader Oishi even divorced his faithful wife and began living with women of poor repute to emphasize the apparent depth of his insouciant degradation.

Convinced at last they were no longer watched or suspected, the vassals—now numbering forty-seven—trekked through the snow on the cold night of December, 14, 1702, to Lord Kira's mansion in Ryogoku in Edo, surrounded the establishment, and attacked. Finding Kira cowering in an out-house, they slew him, cut off his head, and walked back across Edo to lay the head before the tombstone of their master, in Sengakuji Temple.

Their punishment, like that of Lord Asano, was ritual self-disembowelment, which was carried out on February 4, 1703. The youngest ronin was only 15; the oldest was 77.

These men are still revered in Japan as faithful retainers

who gave up their homes and their lives to avenge their lord and to bring about justice in the true spirit of the Japanese warrior.

A less well-known but nonetheless remarkable true story is that of the *Byakko-tai* or White Tiger Unit of Aizu Wakamatsu, the fiefdom of Lord Takamori Matsudaira. It was during the final days of the War of Restoration, in 1868. The Shogun had already agreed to relinquish the reins of control to the Emperor, but a few supporters of the Shogun continued to fight on, here and there. One of these pockets of resistence was in Aizu Wakamatsu, its stronghold being the Tsurugajo Castle.

The White Tiger Unit was a band of 37 boys, all 15 or 16 years of age, who had sworn an oath to defend the castle and Lord Takamori to the death. As the Imperial Forces neared and began to surround the city, the White Tigers fired their scanty supply of ammunition, then fell back.

Later, seeing flames rising from the castle, they assumed their lord's stronghold had fallen to the enemy and so determined to carry out their oath.

One boy named Shinoda stabbed himself in the stomach. Two more named Nagase and Hayashi plunged their swords into each other's chests. A fourth fell on his sword. And so it went until all twenty were down. (Nineteen died, the twentieth survived.)

The day was September 23, 1868. The place was Iimoriyama, outside Aizu Wakamatsu.

Several years ago, while I was engaged in research for a book I was writing in Japan, I happened to visit an ancient temple, the Toshoji, in Kamakura, where the priest acquainted me with a story that I think must be one of the most wondrous in all suicide annals. It was so fantastic that I could not accept it without further substantiation, so that same week I visited four museums and libraries in Kamakura, until I was at last satisfied that this story was not merely an old priest's imaginative maundering.

The seacoast town of Kamakura was the seat of government in Japan in the 1300's. The Emperor, cloistered in Kyoto, did not rule. The Shogun—the exalted "barbarian-subduing generalissimo"—had set up his *bakufu* or military-camp government far to the east in Kamakura to keep his samurai from catching and falling ill with the effete manners of the court, but he too at length surrendered his authority to a line of regents: the Hojo family.

One of the Hojos, Takatoki, held the reins of power in Japan on the fifth of July in 1333, when his capital was besieged by General Yoshisada Nitta, an adherent to the Imperial cause. By evening of the day in question, it had become evident that the Regent Takatoki's army was defeated. A strange man who is best remembered in Japan today because of his fondness for the hundreds of dogs he kept in princely style, Takatoki quickly decided what it was that he then must do.

First, he had his wife and child disguised as fisherfolk and smuggled out of his beleaguered capital in a fishing boat bound for the island of Oshima. Next, he announced his own intentions to his followers, many of whom insisted on being allowed to accompany him that evening.

At length a long procession left the same temple where I first heard this story and walked through the evening dark in a northeasterly direction, toward the low hills that ring much of Kamakura. Every fifth man or so carried a torch, giving the line of march the appearance of an elongated, slowly-crawling glow-worm. At the outskirts of the capital, the road they were following began to climb along the slope of the first hill, becoming a narrow, winding path that fell off sharply into a brush-filled ravine to their left and below. While most of the men were still strung out along this track, the head of the procession reached the large cave to which Takatoki had been leading them.

The cave resembled a room that had been half cut away and exposed (it is still that way today, over six hundred years later), and an overhanging cliff made it appear roomier than it actually was. Under the ledge of this cliff Takatoki halted, even as a soft mist began to fall. Some of his followers gathered around him, while others crowded back into the cave, but the majority remained standing along the path behind and below their ruler.

Takatoki spoke briefly to an old retainer beside him, who passed the message on down the line. The men carrying torches, which were now beginning to sputter in the gradually increasing rain, stuck them upright into the soft earth beside the path. Then they all began to make their preparations, Takatoki himself removing his outer robe and unsheathing his short sword.

At that instant a commotion was heard from below. Soon a young girl of striking beauty appeared hastily pushing past the men standing in her way. Crying "Wait! Wait!," she rushed up to Takatoki and threw herself down at his feet.

"Master," she sobbed, "take me with you. Please!"

For a moment, the austere tension eased off Takatoki's face. The girl was his mistress, whom he was said to love far more than his wife. (He had sent his wife and son to safety so the Hojo family line would not be broken.) He touched her bowed head lightly, then nodded to a retainer poised behind her, who drew his knife and deftly cut the lovely girl's throat, severing the carotid arteries.

The others returned calmly to the business at hand.

Although Takatoki had been a wastrel much of his life, he now showed no weakness of spirit or purpose whatsoever. Kneeling among his followers, he quickly made the

prescribed stomach-cut across his abdomen and then
signalled for a retainer to finish the job. The retainer
inexpertly cut too deep, and Takatoki's head rolled away,
completely severed from the trunk of his body.

His followers took their cue from their liege lord. With
no hesitation, half of them knelt and made the gash across
their abdomens, while the other half served as assistants
and chopped off their heads. Then half of those still alive
knelt and sliced themselves open below the waist and were
in turn decapitated. At the end, of course, a few remained
who had to make their own stomach-cuts deep enough to
let their lives spill out through them.

A group of servants who had accompanied the procession stood back in the shadows at a respectful distance
watching in dumbfounded silence this bloody event, which
was to become known as the "night of the mass hara-kiri at
Kamakura." It was they who carried the report of what
had happened there to the incredulous General Nitta.

As the closing curtain descended, the servants saw the
last of the torches sputter out in the rain and heard the
intermittent sounds of several of the heads that were slowly
working their way down the slope from the path above,
catching now and again on a rock or bush but then rolling
on.

What they witnessed during those few brief minutes
along that torch-lit path had been the self-sought death of
Takatoki's mistress and the suicides by hara-kiri of Takatoki Hojo and no less than eight hundred and seventy-
three Hojo warriors and retainers.

Crime and Punishment in
Two Countries,

In which chapter the author comes across as a liberal-hating conservative, as well as a racist.

These days many Westerners are dismayed and puzzled by rampant crime in their home countries. In particular, this is true of the United States, where 80 c/o of reported crimes goes unsolved and where, by some estimates, only about five percent of all crimes are reported.

In Japan, on the other hand, almost all crimes are reported, so the figures about felonies there are all the more amazing.

With twice Japan's population, we suffer from 215 times more robberies, 10 times more murders, and 25 times more rapes than they do.

While in the U.S. one in every five households is a victim of crime at least once a year, Japanese pedestrians walk safely anywhere by day or night, lost cash and other valuables are handed over to the authorities as a matter of routine, and no one bothers to count his change.

According to INTERPOL, Japan has the lowest crime rate in the world, although certain crimes are on the rise, possibly due to the rising living standard.

Why are the Japanese so law-abiding?

Ministry of Justice officials attribute it to a common language (so why are we promoting bilingual education in the U.S.?), cultural solidarity—or social cohesion, strict gun controls, a high level of literacy and education, and lack of a land border that criminals can easily cross to escape. They have a strong family system in which wrongdoing by a single member brings shame and disgrace to all. When the Red Army terrorists tried to shoot their way out of a siege by the police, the father of one of the radicals committed suicide.

Also responsible is the traditional respect of the Japanese for authority. When a rioting mob protesting the war in Vietnam rampaged through the center of Kyoto, a single traffic policeman faced the onrush and calmly raised his hand at a red traffic light. The mob stopped dead in its tracks.

When a study was made of the students participating in riots, it was found that almost no athletes were represented, giving rise to the theory that rioting was merely a way to burn off excess youthful energy.

In Japan, most criminal cases are tried before three judges who, sitting together, decide the question of innocence or guilt, and this system seems to work very well. Former Chief Justice of the United States, Warren Earl Burger, also questioned the principle of trial by jury, and was quoted in TIME as saying, "if we could eliminate the jury, we would save a lot of time. You can try a case without a jury in one day that would take you a week or two weeks with a jury."

Japan did experiment with trial by jury during the years between 1928 and 1943. The accused were given the right to choose between jury trial and trial by judges. The number who chose the former averaged only thirty a year during that fifteen-year period, almost all of the accused evidently preferring *not* to be judged by their peers, so jury trials were abandoned.

The absence of trial by jury is one of the weightiest reasons why many Americans watched uneasily when the U.S. Armed Forces, in October of 1953, gave Japanese courts primary jurisdiction over military men and their dependents for offenses committed off-base in Japan. They were worried that the Japanese, perhaps still smarting from their defeat in the war, might take advantage of their new power to punish American offenders more severely than their offenses warranted.

They need not have been concerned. Japanese courts bent over backwards to show leniency to Americans haled before them. In numerous instances, they were so forgiving that they let go scot-free culprits who deserved at least some manner of punishment, and our military prosecutors had to seek out other charges (to avoid double jeopardy) with which to bring these men to even lesser justice.

By May of 1957, three and a half years later, when the bulk of our forces had left Japan, the Japanese police had apprehended 27,000 U.S. citizens, of which number they indicted only 500 (an arrest-indictment rate much lower than that for their own countrymen.) Approximately half of the 27,000 were for traffic violations, of which only eleven were prosecuted.

Of the 500 indicted, thirty percent were punished only with fines—and small ones at that. At the end of this time, e.g., May of 1957, only thirty-seven American citizens were serving sentences in Japanese prisons, none of which exceeded fifteen years in length. The death sentence was never meted out to an American, although more than a few Americans had killed Japanese under a variety of circumstances.

The U.S. Department of State confirmed in a Senate hearing that American offenders generally got lighter sentences from Japanese courts than they would have received from our own and went on to testify that the Japanese had built a special jail for the confinement of Americans that was "far above" the standard for Japanese prisons.

One of the most bizarre mass murders and bank robberies in Japanese crime annals took place in a small suburban bank in Tokyo on the twenty-sixth of January, 1948. It still arouses large numbers of Japanese to heights of furious emotion and is more of a cause celebre in that country than the case of Caryl Chessman was in the U.S.

At about three-thirty in the afternoon of the above date, a middle-aged man with a scar on his face appeared in the Shiina-machi branch of the Teikoku Bank in Toshima Ward in Tokyo. He was wearing red boots (not as uncommon in Japan as they would be here) and an armband identifying him as a "technical official" from the Toshima Ward Office. He asked to see the branch manager.

The branch manager being out, the visiting "official" was taken to the desk of the manager's assistant, to whom he showed a business card that further identified him as a medical doctor.

"There has been an outbreak of dysentery in this neighborhood," he told the assistant manager, " and a man who now has the sickness tells us that he has come to this bank several times recently. Will you please assemble all your employees? I must ask you to take preventive measures against dysentery."

The doors of the bank had just been closed for the day, so the assistant called the other fifteen employees of the bank together to hear the "ward-office doctor" explain what had to be done.

Very carefully the man in the red boots laid out sixteen doses of medicine, in the form of white powder, and asked that each employee fill his own tea cup with water. He cautioned them that the medicine could have a harmful effect on the enamel of their teeth so they should place the dose on their tongues carefully and swallow it all down with one gulp of water.

At the doctor's signal, all sixteen employees picked up their cups and followed his instructions to the letter.

Almost immediately they began to feel tearing internal

pains and then staggered off toward the water-cooler, where they all collapsed in quick succession. Of the sixteen bank employees, twelve died.

The man in the red boots gathered up ¥164,000 and a few checks, then fled.

On the twenty-first of August, one Sadamichi Hirasawa, a fifty-seven-year old artist living in the city of Otaru in northern Japan, was picked up as a suspect. In jail, he first tried to commit suicide and then, on the twenty-seventh of September, he admitted giving a derivative of prussic acid to the sixteen employees of the Teikoku Bank.

Although he later denied having admitted guilt, Hirasawa was sentenced to death, whereupon began an almost comically long series of appeals, stays of execution, reversals, retrials, and signature-gathering campaigns. He died in 1987, still in prison.

Considering their success in other areas of crime-fighting, it seems strange to find there are in Japan 110,000 *yakuza* (gangsters) who are members of Japan's seven major, 25–30 medium-sized, and hundreds of smaller independent criminal organizations. The *Yamaguchi-gumi*, with 10,800 members, is without question the largest and most closely knit band of procurers, gamblers, extortionists, and hoodlums (the Japanese like to call them *machi no shirami* or lice of the town) in the world today.

In assorted illicit ways, these *yakuza* earn some five billion dollars yearly. They send high-priced call girls out on whoring missions, manage floating (marked) card and (loaded) dice games, and extort money from corporate officials for sexual indiscretions and non-payment of taxes.

They are often identifiable by their dark glasses, tattoos (if visible), garish outfits (reminiscent of the cast of "Guys and Dolls"), and missing joints of their little fingers, which they cut off in apology for mistaken words or actions. They borrowed this custom from the brothels of Edo, where sometimes a 'spring-selling' denizen would lop off a joint or two to suggest the depth of her feelings for her true heart of the moment.

The *yakuza* and their bands trace their origin to the civil strife of the early 1600s, about the time the Tokugawa Shogunate was beginning to take form.

Chobei Banzuin, a Robin Hood-like character, assembled, from among one-time bandits, the mighty labor force that built Edo Castle for the Tokugawas. These workers were content to let Chobei run things as long as he let them gamble to the content of their hearts. What he asked in return, in addition to hard work, was that the laborers swear fealty to him and obey the the Code of the *Yakuza* (purportedly knights who rescued the distressed and protected the weak) he had begun to formulate.

Chobei allowed some of his followers to set up their own sub-bands. Often these served as spies for the magistrates and even acted as auxiliary police forces in times of emergency. Later, during the struggle between the Imperial and Shogunate forces just prior to the restoration of the Emperor Meiji, both sides competed for *yakuza* allegiance. The former offered the gangsters samurai status, while the latter held out the promise of remission of debts and taxes. Thus was built the foundation of the oddly close cooperation and mutual tolerance in Japan, extending even to the present day, of those law supportive and those law disruptive.

Even more important to the continued existence of the *yakuza* than the tolerance of the gendarmerie, however, is their time-honored scruple against harming or even disturbing the average citizen. In fact, a director of the *Yamaguchi-gumi* states that his band's role is to protect the citizens at night, while the police protect them during the day.

In the offices of the *Yamaguchi-gumi* are displayed copies of the oath their *yakuza* must take. It commits them to courteous actions, respect for the elderly, striving for self-betterment, an humble attitude, and devotion to the prosperity of their society.

The lip-service paid by the the *yakuza* to the spirit of *ninkyō* (chivalry) is such that many Japanese doubt the 'lice of the town' can ever be dislodged from their position in Japan's society. A further enhancement to their reputation, at least in the eyes of many, is their strong stance against the forces of Communism. Once when leftist demonstrators massed to protest and forestall the visit to Japan of President Eisenhower, Yoshio Kodama, one of Japan's top *kuromaku* (underworld movers and shakers), recruited 19,000 *yakuza* and 11,000 *yakuza*-controlled street vendors to confront the leftists.

On December 6, 1968, the manager of the Kokubunji Branch (on the western outskirts of Tokyo) of the Nihon Shintaku Bank received an extortion note. He was ordered to leave three million yen ($8,333) in a certain place at a specified time. Otherwise, the note warned, his home in Tokyo would be blown up.

The branch manager did not comply, but he informed the employees at his bank of the threat.

Four days later, in the morning, four employees left the same bank in a Cedric car and started out for the Toshiba factory in Fuchu, a few miles south. They were carrying something of considerable bulk and value: three hundred million yen.

Japanese companies customarily give bonuses to their employees twice a year: at the end of June and at the end of December. But many like Toshiba were passing out the year-end bonuses fairly early in December this year, to give their employees more time for their New Year's shopping. Usually the bonuses equalled about one month's wages but sometimes ranged as high as two or three months'. It was the bonus money for Toshiba's Fuchu factory workers that the four bank clerks were delivering that morning. And it was all in cash; Japanese companies don't pay salaries or bonuses by check.

At nine o'clock, as the Cedric was driving down the road that goes past Fuchu Prison, a uniformed patrolman on the familiar white motorcycle of the police forces waved the bank car over to the side of the road. The patrolman, whose face was largely concealed by his helmet and scarf, hurried over to the halted vehicle.

"We've just had a call from the police station in Sugamo," he said tersely. "The home of your branch manager has been blown up."

Sugamo was the district of Tokyo in which the branch manager resided.

"And we've learned," the patrolman went on, "that there's a charge of dynamite planted somewhere in this car. It's set to go off any minute now." He began at once to inspect the car.

In less time than it takes to tell it, the four bank clerks were out of the Cedric and running for the ditch, completely forgetting the money entrusted to their care. As they threw themselves into the presumed safety of that declivity, the patrolman climbed in behind the wheel of their car and drove off with the three hundred million yen.

Perhaps it is needless to say that the man who had made off with the largest cash haul in Japan's history was not a genuine policeman. At the date of this writing, they still have not found out just who he was. And the statute of limitations has expired.

Despite the above implication, the efficiency of the Japanese police represents a primal reason for the low rate of crime in that country. On the whole, they are capable, dedicated men and women. And there are fewer of them. (Japan has one policeman for every 729 inhabitants, while the U.S. has one for every 502 and France has one for every 347).

Further, they are often emasculated by inadequate and outdated laws. For example, Japan has no law that specifically provides for punishment of criminals convicted of kidnapping for ransom, which is a crime only recently imported. It has no law against espionage. It has no law against incest. It has no treaty of extradition with any country but the U.S. It has no law against statutory rape. (Forcible violation of a girl under thirteen years of age is, however, a crime.) Unless he has a warrant of arrest or sees the man actually engaged in an offense, the policeman is not authorized to search a suspicious person for weapons. If he uses force in apprehending any member of a mob, the policeman risks prosecution for attempted murder, false arrest, or inflicting bodily injury. (Labor, student, and leftist organizations are alert for such opportunities to harass the gendarmes.) Only in a state of national emergency, which has not been proclaimed since the end of World War II, can the police use force to subdue unruly demonstrators, which explains in part the mob violence and wild abandonment of the Sixties.

Hampered though they are by comparatively small numbers and by certain legal restrictions, the Japanese police turn in a very creditable performance. In a recent year, they secured convictions in 83 percent of all armed robberies, 90 percent of rapes, and 95 percent of all murders, while, in the same year, the police of Tokyo fired a total of only four shots from their firearms, two of them in to the air.

That the Japanese police have functioned so well in a milieu of strong protection of civil rights is a tribute to their suberb training, technical sophistication, and neighborhood organization.

Competition for police jobs is strenuous. In an average year, only one in ten applicants is accepted. All must have graduated from high school, while the percentage who have graduated from college is forty—and rising. Top positions in the police forces are filled by outstanding graduates of the best universities who pass a very tough senior public official employment examination. Only 20 or so pass this test each year, but these receive rapid promotions and in the early part of their careers serve in other government ministries and in major embassies abroad to vary their experience.

A few years ago, the chief of the Tokyo Metropolitan Police Forces visited major U.S. cities and was astounded to see no policemen walking through the neighborhoods. In Japan, the *o-mawari-san* or Mr. Walk Around is a familiar fixture of the local scene, as is the *kōban* from which he operates.

The *kōban* or 'box' (actually a small building with communications equipment and a place to sleep and eat) is manned around the clock by *o-mawari-san* assigned for two or three years to one neighborhood.

In Japan, there are 16,000 *kōban* or an average of one for every 6,900 residents. In cities like Tokyo, one patrolman keeps tabs on about 300 households, visiting each once or twice a year and getting to know the inhabitants.

Because of the *kōban* system, the excellent communications network, and the black and white patrol cars, the average time of the Tokyo police in responding to emergency calls is only three minutes and 23 seconds.

So good, in fact, are the Japanese police in apprehending those who commit what they call 'atrocious crimes' that two of their major headaches these days are bicycle thefts and public urination (by men), the latter accounting for most of the minor offenses in a nation of law-abiders.

The problem is that for centuries urination in the fields was encouraged since it contributed, in a small way, to replenishing the supply of water without which the wet-paddy rice could not grow. Because of this, Japanese men came to consider it an inalienable right to urinate wherever and whenever they wished.

In the bar districts of the major cities it has been no uncommon sight for five or ten or even more men to be lined up in a street or alleyway relieving themselves, oblivious to the consternation of the passing public, who at last began to complain, as did foreign visitors (especially women).

/a   I recall an American women named Peg Bennett, then in her forties, who worked with me in Osaka in 1948 and 1949. Peg was a sub-section chief in our postal censorship section and worked in the post office building near Osaka Station. Once day she chanced to look out her window and see a Japanese man squatting down and defecating in the gutter across the street.

Shocked and horrified, Peg flew to the main entrance of the post office building where she collared one of the Japanese guards we employed and dragging him behind her, ran across the street to the squatting, oblivious man. "Make him stop!" Peg yelled at the guard, who in turn shouted, "Stop that!" at the squatting man.

The task, however, which this particular individual had undertaken was one that was not so easy to cut off in mid-course. He had little choice but to press on with the business at hand.

"Make him stop!" ordered the frantic Peg. "How?" asked the confused guard. "Hit him! Hit him!" shouted Peg, keenly aware that a crowd was gathering and regarding her with interest.

In those early days, the word of an Occupationaire, male or female, was Holy Writ, so the poor guard pulled out his nightstick, his only weapon, and began to beat the defecator about the shoulders and on the back. This may have hastened the business at hand but did not terminate it entirely, for there were still some essential tidying-up operations to be taken care of.

At last, this accomplished, the hapless Japanese man, perhaps still wondering what it was he had done wrong, rose to his feet, buckled his belt, and bowed first to Peg, then to the guard and loped off.

One factor in their success in repressing crime is the realistic and practical way in which the Japanese deal with drug offenders.

Their first antidrug law, adopted in the 1880's, prescribed decapitation for those caught trafficking in narcotics. Today they give out life sentences for those convicted of selling heroin and begin each addict's treatment "cold turkey," without chemical crutches such as methadone, and the number of addicts is small (but growing).

Whenever Japanese success in dealing with crime and meting out punishment is brought up, admiring mention is usually also made of their gun-control law.

Private possession of handguns was banned by the U.S. Occupation Forces soon after their entry into Japan, and Japan has never rescinded it. The estimates of the number of handguns in illegal Japanese hands today do not exceed 30,000—a "mosquito's teardrop," as the Japanese would say, in comparison to the 100,000,000 estimated to be in the U.S. The city of Atlanta, which is 55% black, is believed to have enough handguns in its boundaries to furnish two to every child, woman, and man living there.

Although the Japanese military forces used rifles and pistols well enough during times of armed hostility, firearms—in the samurai heart of the Japanese—have never really been their weapons of choice. They were first introduced into Japan in 1542 by the Portugese, who had landed on the island of Tanegashima off the southern coast of Kyushu.

The governor of the island, Lord Tokitaka, watched the Portugese shoot fowl with their firearms. Hugely impressed, he was at length able to buy one for 2,000 *ryō*- a very considerable sum. He tried to buy more, to no avail.

Why is this Texan telling us this? (And why am I telling whoever will read this that he is a Texan?)

He asked how to make them. The captain of the vessel, Mendez Pinto, could not—or would not—enlighten him.

Tokitaka summoned Koshiro Shinokawa, one of his vassals, to his presence and ordered him to bend all efforts to copy the Portugese musket. Considerable time was spent on this endeavor without notable success until at last another ship visited Tanegashima with a sailor with some experience as a gunsmith aboard. A man named Kimpei, another of the island lord's retainers, was able, by crook and hook, to learn much from him about the making of firearms: all that he needed to know, in fact, except how to make the trigger device and the mechanism for locking the gunbarrel. Here he ran up against a stone wall. The Portugese ex-gunsmith decided he had already given away too much for too little.

Kimpei asked the sailor what more he wanted. While the sailor was pondering his answer, his wandering eyes fell on Kimpei's lovely daughter Wakasa.

"Her," he answered, pointing at Wakasa.

"You ask too much," Kimpei said in refusal.

Wakasa, however, was of a different mind. Overflowing with filial piety and devotion to her native land, she volunteered to accompany the barbarian to his distant home. Voila. Kimpei was taught the final secret. His daughter sailed off to the west, to be lost to history but not forgotten, for a monument to her filial piety stands today on the island of Tanegashima.

Within a year, Kimpei was able to manufacture 60 European-style muskets of good quality.

Over the succeeding years, the Japanese used firearms widely and effectively, but the point of this digression is that eventually the Japanese national stomach turned against the use of firearms because, in warfare, a musket made a peasant the equal of a samurai. This was intolerable, so during most of the 17th and 18th centuries and well into the 19th, during the Pax Tokugawa, the firearms of the

Japanese rusted and gathered dust, their magnificent swords, superior even to the blades of Damascus and Toledo, being the weapons of choice.

Although the sword is more difficult to conceal on the person than the handgun, it is still used frequently enough by the gangs of Japan—and the shorter swords, such as the one that killed Inejiro Asanuma, leader of the Socialist Party in 1960, in particular.

Today, if you watch the Japanese 'police-versus-the-wicked' movies, you will see a plethora of handguns in use; so many, in fact, you may conclude the pistol is an obligatory accessory to the *yakuza*, together with the tattoo and the truncated little finger and the dark glasses. Whether these movies are a reflection of reality or mere fantasy is a moot question.

Another moot question is whether or not strict gun control laws have actually contributed to a lower incidence of crime in Japan. And, more to the next point, whether or not such a law would contribute to a reduction in crime in the United States.

In 1911, New York passed the Sullivan Law, which was the strictest handgun control regulation in the U.S. until Washington passed an even more stringent law much more recently. These laws did nothing to prevent the murder of John Lennon in New York City or the attempted assassination of Ronald Reagan in Washington, D.C.

Apparently there exists in the United States a very sizable amount of knee-jerk opposition to handguns. The mere mention of the word is enough to drive these opponents into a form of hysteria, during which they utterly lose their powers of ratiocination. They demand that handguns be taken away from the citizenry. (If voluntarily, the law-abiding would turn in theirs, while the law-resistors would cherish and cling to their own all the more.) If confiscatory, then a thorough search of every and each dwelling in this country—together with all barns, outhouses, woodsheds, and nearby woods—would be required. (Manifestly, a labor of Hercules.) Failing that, they would have all handguns registered. (How would that change anything? The law-abiding would still use theirs in self-defense, while the wicked and evil ones would pull the trigger in moments of deliberate mayhem, then toss the weapon in a deep river and say it was lost or stolen.)

Of the many millions of handguns now in private hands, perhaps one in every 250 is used yearly for criminal purposes. The other 249 harm no one but serve to enhance self-defense measures. Why do some get more exercised over those 249 weapons than over the one used to kill or rob? When will the focus shift from weapons to the people who use weapons illegally?

The bottom line is that the American people are frightened to the depths of their souls by the crescive wave of violent crime in their country, and they have lost confidence in the ability of the police to protect them. Therefore, they reason, they must protect themselves; hence, the booming sales of handguns, guard dogs, and burglary protective devices. In Florida recently the legislature passed, over the governor's veto and the perfervid opposition of liberal opponents of hand-carried pistols, a law permitting motorists to carry concealed pistols, rifles, and shotguns in their cars for self-defense. The measure was passed 125–27, almost five to one.

In Washington, D.C., with its declining population and the toughest gun control law in the country, the number of robberies with handguns actually doubled last year.

Another reason for the success of the police in Japan is the astounding degree of cooperation accorded them by the public, which is surprising in view of the harsh repression of the 1920's and 1930's and the traces of police arrogance that, unfortunately, still remain. (A hangover from Japan's feudal era, which was characterized by the Japanese expression *Kanson Mimpi,* meaning "Respect officialdom; despise the common man.") A recent survey of three thousand citizens showed that sixty percent of them looked upon the policeman as "a kind and warm-hearted friend in times of need," while twenty-three percent replied that they had no complaint at all against the police.

The Japanese may be winning their fight against crime, but on the other side of the Pacific, in a country where an adult burglar runs only one chance in 412 of going to prison for any single job (for juveniles, the ratio is one in 659), we are losing ours. Clearly and without any question. At this stage in our national development, we are faced with a choice between dispensing justice and dispensing with it, and it looks as if we have opted for the latter.

All along the pipeline to the statue of the blindfolded lady with the scales in her hand, everyone involved is underachieving. They are failing to do the jobs expected of them: the police, prosecutors, judges, and prison officials.

And the public. While we are scared stiff of what is happening, we lack, as a people, the will to take decisive action. We will not vote the funds needed to hire more, better-educated policeman. Some cities, like Boston and Los Angeles, have actually been forced to make significant cuts in the number of their policemen due to budgetary restrictions. Nor will we vote for the funds necessary to build larger and more efficient prisons, so that states like Texas and Florida have found it necessary to release hundreds of prisoners before the expiration of their terms. At the same time we have allowed the liberal madmen among us to pass laws that enshrine for enforced adulation the rights of those dedicated to the pursuit of crime for its own sake and abuse of law-enforcement agencies and judicial institutions with tactics designed to confuse, delay, obfuscate, and coddle, with the result that most criminals have no fear or respect whatsoever for the crime-prevention system.

Our criminals know that today there is very little chance

of their being punished for any particular crime. Our police make arrests in only a small fraction of the cases in their files. Our prosecutors reject or water down the charges against 50 to 80 percent of the few who are arrested. Once in court, the number actually convicted is smaller still. In New York City, for instance, only one in 200 serious crimes leads to a prison sentence more than one year in length, and even that may be shortened by pardon or parole.

In 1776 there were no municipal police forces and almost no prisons in the United States. Even in Boston, the hotbed of agitation for rebellion against the Crown, the mobs— many of whose members also sat on local juries and in town meetings—were so domesticated that they would not riot on Saturdays or Sundays. Crime in those times for the most part involved moral and religious offenses instead of illegal acts of an acquisitive or violent nature.

But, however slowly, the incidence of crime did increase, as did the measures to cope with it. From 1776 until the present day, punishment—usually erratic and inconsistent—wended its way through stages of severity until the 20th century when bits and pieces of a new outlook on crime and punishment began to win support. Among them were the idea that in general punishment had been too severe, that punishment—including the capital variety —did not really deter crime, that society should dedicate itself to rehabilitation instead of punishment of the criminal, that poverty and unemployment bred crime, that society itself ("We have met the enemy, and they are us") is to blame, and that the criminal, by and large, is more to be pitied than blamed.

Then the tsunami-like crime wave of the Sixties began. (Violent crime has *quad*rupled since then.) As the tsunami inundated us, beliefs about some of the old saws were disproved before our unbelieving eyes. "Crime never pays," they told us in church and in school. Nonsense. Today crime pays—and pays handsomely. "Murder will out," they pontificated. Tommyrot. In New York City, nearly forty percent of the murderers are never caught and punished. Of the 976 gangland murders committed in the Chicago area during the sixty-year period beginning in 1919, only two murderers were convicted.

Also crumbling or being subjected to close scrutiny were some of the concepts foisted on us by 20th-century liberalism.

Item, that poverty and unemployment are the root causes of crime. If so, ask the interrogators, why then did rates of robbery and burglary decline during the 1930s, the time of our worst depression, and increase during the 1960s, a time of general prosperity?

Expanding their mental horizons, more than a few crime experts are now suggesting crime may not be linked to social conditions nearly to the extent previously envisioned but rather springs from other impulses. In 1949, Barnes and Teeter analyzed the causes and found that "Most offenses are committed through greed, not need." Former Attorney General William Saxbe has said, "I believe a great many offenders commit crimes because they want to commit crimes."

Supporting the theory of greed are the studies of French sociologist Emile Durkheim who found that great bursts of crime occur when prosperity unleashes overweening ambition.

Item, drugs are a root cause, and drug addiction should be treated like any other illness, with sympathetic medical treatment. Yet a study made in New York City, with as much if not more drug abuse than any other city, found the majority of violent street crime is *not* committed by drug addicts.

Item, that criminals are mostly abused, underprivileged, sometimes mentally disturbed persons of little education and low mental capacity. When terrible crimes, including the assassinations of well-known persons, are committed, we rush to the judgment that "they must be crazy," as if we cannot cope with the thought that anyone of intelligence in the range of normality could do such a thing. Yet studies of prison populations have shown the inmates to be equal to the general public in intelligence tests, and since they are where they are, one has to assume the criminals outside the prison walls are even smarter, since they haven't been caught.

Item, that capital punishment does not deter violent crime: the stoutest plank in the platform of the Weeping Hearts. In support of this, they pointed triumphantly to the fact that in jurisdictions where capital punishment had been abolished, there had followed no immediate, sharp increase in capital crimes—while ignoring the fact that in those same jurisdictions, even when the death penalty had been carried on the books, it had seldom, if at all, been imposed for many years.

Now sophisticated research is finding that, to paraphrase Lord Acton, punishment does deter, and absolute punishment deters absolutely. For, whatever the worth of other arguments con the death sentence, no one, no matter how purblind, can argue that death imposed by society does not at least deter that one murderer from killing anyone else.

But, the argument runs, execution of a murderer is nothing more than society's vengeance. And what, the right-thinker asks in rebuttal, is wrong with vengeance? Society need not be ashamed for feeling anger about crime and desiring vengeance against criminals. These are virtuous sentiments that express a natural, life-enhancing moral order. ("Vengeance is mine," saith the Lord, and if He would only come down to Earth and smite the wicked hip and thigh, we might be justified in leaving such punishment in His hands, but the only grapes being trampled these days seem to be in the vineyards of

Merely that the latter part of the book Bible-thumpers thump frowns upon, it should be enough in a country like the US.

California and western New York and not in the land of Wrath.)

Item, that crime is an activity in which all ethnic groups participate, more or less in equal proportion to their numbers.

Absolute balderdash. Crime in late 20th-century America is mostly a function of the Negroes, who, with only eleven percent of the population, are responsible for 37 percent of the assaults, 48 percent of the murders, manslaughters, and rapes, and 57 percent of all robberies. In the cities, they commit 60 percent of the rapes and two out of every three robberies.

Item, that there is no such thing as a bad boy. However monstrous his crime, he is still a good candidate for rehabilitation, given Christian patience and time. But there *are* bad boys—and girls, and some of them are very, very bad indeed.

Beguiled by this fatuity, our courts have never really considered that a child could be a criminal. Mischievous and irresponsible perhaps—but not a true criminal. Consequently, an underage felon is usually not photographed and seldom fingerprinted. His records are treated as confidential and are destroyed when he becomes a legal adult. And, although more than half of all serious crimes are now committed by youths between the ages of ten and 17, we treat their delinquency, in the words of James Higgins, a juvenile judge in New Haven, "as a civil inquiry into the doings of a child," with resulting light punishments that certainly do *not* fit their crimes.

In a heterogeneous nation like the U.S., the pluralism of ethnic groups promotes alienation and creates "subcultures of violence," in which there is, says Sociologist Marvin Wolfgang, "quick resort to physical combat as a measure of daring, courage or defense of status that appears to be a cultural expression." (Witness the Puerto

Rican, Negro, and Italian street gangs of New York City.)

Item, that the criminal should be rehabilitated, more heed should be paid to the rehabilitation of the criminal than to his punishment (society's vengeance), that society is in desperate need of his good will and competent services once he is restored to his proper senses and retrained to let the good that is in all men shine forth.

Perhaps the whole concept of criminal rehabilitation took shape at times when there was a shortage of hands and minds, at a time when more people were desperately needed to conquer the wilderness, fight the Redskins, throw back Attila the Hun, sail unexplored seas, and convert the heathen masses. Perhaps. But whenever it was and for whatever reason it came about, it has seen its day. The problem today is over-population, not a shortage of people.

Anyway, we are now reaching the iconoclastic conclusion that prisons cannot rehabilitate criminals. After release, 70 percent of them again commit crimes. Many experimental studies conclude that no matter whether efforts at rehabilitation take the form of probation or parole, academic or vocational training, group or individual counselling, psychiatric treatment, or short or long sentences, they don't work. After studying hundreds of such programs for 20 years, Columbia Sociologist Robert Martinson concluded, "The prison that makes every effort at rehabilitation succeeds no better than the prison that leaves its inmates to rot." Criminologist Hans Mattick believes that "The prisons have become largely drama schools which force people to act as if they were rehabilitated along stereotyped conventions."

Because of prison conditions and because prisoners regard their imprisonment not as their just deserts, but as society's unwarranted violation of their rights and interference with their freedom of movement, a great many felons leave prison seething with an antisocial rage that quickly erupts in more felonies.

It seems we must finally face up to the realization it is naive to assume we can alter the character of a convict who has happily spent much of his life in hot pursuit of wicked behavior.

The temptation is strong to press for a wider application of the death penalty with all executions being shown on prime-time television. Or for an adoption of the old Japanese punishment called *gokumon*.

Upon being sentenced to death, the commoner was led out through the gate of the court (called the *jigoku-mon* or Gate to Hell) to the place of execution where he was bound and held by three outcasts (*Eta*). After the Lord Chief Executioner had beheaded him, his head was washed and carried to either Kozukabara in Asakusa or to Suzugamori in Shinagawa, both places in Edo.

There the head was nailed to a board for three days, with the details of the crime written on a piece of paper pasted below. After the head was taken down, the paper itself was left there for another 27 days.

But sober reflection suggests we do not have the *dokyō* (stomach, nerve) for it. So perhaps, as French criminologist Jean Lacassagne said long ago, "A society gets the criminals it deserves."

Thanks to most of this chapter an otherwise fun book has gone to hell.

What—and How—the Japanese Drink

According to Shinto mythology, the gods who created Japan were surpassingly fond of Liquid Solace, and the Japanese have never found any solid reason not to follow their divine lead. (It stuns the imagination to contemplate what the Christian world—where a lot of stout-hearted fellows are already putting in enough plucky work with their elbows to keep the breweries working nights—might be like today if the Holy Scriptures told us that Jesus and His Disciples used to hang around a Jerusalem cocktail lounge most evenings getting disorderly and glassy-eyed.)

During the Han and Wei dynasties, Chinese historians who visited Japan (before the Japanese had a written language of their own) recorded that "the people of Wa (Japan) are much given to strong drink."

But it is written elsewhere that until the beginning of the Nara Era in the early 700s, sake (pronounced like blase) was supposedly drunk, due to the influence of its first godly imbibers, only at religious rituals, so either there must have been a surfeit of such rituals or else the Japanese had found something besides rice from which to brew intoxicants.

In those desperate times, the newly-harvested rice was chewed by virgins, when available, of the Shinto shrines and then spat into a vat where an enzyme in their saliva converted the starch in the rice to sugar. (*Kamosu*, the verb meaning 'to brew sake,' comes from *kamu*, the verb for 'to chew.') Then fermentation took over, leading eventually to a cloudy, thick, lumpy alcoholic drink with a vicious kick,

106

producing hang-overs that often required prolonged hospitalization.

Luckily for succeeding generations, a more scientific process was brought from China about A.D. 300, the ancestor of the one still in use today.

In Japan's two oldest books, the *Kojiki* (A.D. 712) and *Nihon Shoki* (A.D. 720), mention is made of *Yashio-ori-no-sake*, which was made from several kinds of fruit, and *Amano-tamu-zake*, which was made from rice. During the Heian Period (A.D. 794-1191), the Japanese were already beginning to drink warmed sake, at least from September until March. Probably someone discovered that heating this intoxicant enhanced the delicate aroma and warmed the body on chilly nights. This was when the *sakazuki* or sake cups began to come in smaller sizes; in larger cups, the liquid too often cooled before it could be consumed.

Although cold sake is now enjoying a revival of popularity, most Japanese drink their sake warm. It is poured into 180 cc. porcelain bottles called *tokkuri* and heated in a pan of hot water on the stove. (U.S.-made baby bottle warmers sold briskly in Japan for several years after someone found that they were ideal for this purpose.) Individual tastes vary, but 110°–120°F. is the preferred range of temperature. The sake is poured from the *tokkuri* into the *sakazuki*—the 18 cc. cup not much larger than a thimble, the bottom of which is placed on the tips of the forefinger and middle finger of the left hand and held in place there with the thumb and same two fingers of the right hand. The drinker should not fill has own cup but only those of others, who will in turn fill his for him, and no one's cup should be filled to the brim.

Exchanging cups is a sake-drinking ritual in which one man first hands his empty cup to another, then fills it for him from a *tokkuri*. The second man immediately drains the cup, rinses it out in a bowl of water provided for that purpose, and returns it to its owner with a bow of his head and then fills it for him. It is the social inferior (in the Japanese sense) who usually initiates this exchange. When one has had enough sake, he may indicate this by turning his cup upside down on the table. Sake is drunk throughout the meal until the rice is served.

Sake (properly called *seishu*) is most often given in English as rice-wine, and it is true that it is similar to wine in alcoholic content (15–17 percent), in the enjoyment of its bouquet, and in the sipping method by which it should be consumed. On the other hand, the process by which it is brewed more nearly resembles that of beer, and it bears further similarity to that drink in that it is generally not aged.

Japan has 3,870 sake breweries that produce 400 million gallons of this social lubricant derived from rice annually in 5,000 brands. Although the breweries are located throughout Japan, Nada and Fushimi are the two areas whose rice-wines are judged the best. Nada, a suburb of Kobe, started producing sake in 1331, but it did not gain national fame for its product until 1840 when it began to use *Miyamizu*, the water found in underground rivers in the city of Nishinomiya just north of Kobe. (Sake is made from water, rice, sake yeast, and pure cultured Koji mold.) Fushimi's sake pre-dates that of Nada, going back to A.D. 794. By and large, Nada's sake is dry (*kara-kuchi*), while that of Fushimi is sweet (*ama-kuchi*).

Sake is judged by how it looks to the eye, how it feels on the tongue, how it smells, and what tastes it leaves in the mouth. Each brand has its own subtle taste distinction, and that too may change with the year as the rice crops vary with the weather. Ideally, its delicate, light flavor complements the basically vegetable and fish make-up of traditional Japanese cuisine.

In addition to the thousands of brands of *seishu* (properly refined sake), there are also *amazake*, a milky sweet beverage pressed from incompletely fermented rice lees, *o-*

toso, the spiced sake drunk at New Year's, and such exotic concoctions as *kikuzake*, which is made with crushed crysanthemum petals.

Unlike the names of wine, which are often geographical in origin, the brands of sake are more, let us say, colorful: *Shirayuki* (White Snow—does it fall in other colors?), *Sawanotsuru* (Swamp Stork), *Nihonzakari* (The Peak of Japan), *Fukumusume* (Happy Maiden), *Hakushika* (White Deer) and *Hakutsuru* (White Stork).

Sake comes in three grades: special (*tokkyū*), first (*ikkyū*), and second (*nikyū*). Nearly one-half of the cost of the special grade goes to the national treasury as taxes, and the tax on spirits ranks third in national importance, after corporation and individual income taxes.

Although the production of sake continues to increase, the Japanese are drinking less of it in comparison to whiskey and beer. In 1937, sake accounted for 68 percent of the country's total liquor consumption, whereas it is now only 30 percent. Several years ago, beer production and consumption passed sake for the first time.

One of the strange misconceptions we Americans hold about sake concerns its potency. According to this popular fallacy, sake packs the wallop of the 151-proof Demerara rum that the British navy uses, diluted copiously with water, to make grog.

Obviously, this is not so. As noted above, sake varies, with the grade, from 15 to 17 percent in alcoholic content, making it only slightly stronger than wine and not nearly as strong as gin, which hovers around the 50 percent mark. (It is about as potent as sherry.) Nor does the warmth of the sake matter much, since the liquid quickly adjusts to body temperature shortly after entering the stomach.

As well as I can determine, this fallacy has its roots in the islands of the Pacific, where American troops found bottles of clear alcoholic liquid among supplies they captured from the Japanese. Some of this was no doubt sake, but most of it was probably *shōchū*, a much stronger drink (to be described later), which would have looked like sake to anyone unable to read the Japanese writing on the label. If it was *shōchū*, and if our soldiers drank it as quickly as I have often seen them swallow such windfalls of liquor (that is, before an officer could "confiscate" it), then it is little wonder that 'sake' earned for itself an undeserved reputation for potency.

Although sake is very mild, I usually awaken the next morning with a slight hang-over after drinking it. At many Japanese-style dinners, the host, in his expansive generosity, will have sake, beer, and Scotch placed on the table so that each guest can have his preference, but the trouble comes with the cup-exchanging ritual. The man on your right may offer you the Scotch he has been drinking, after which the man on your left may offer you beer. And then a geisha refills your *sakazuki* with sake. It is difficult, if not downright rude, to refuse these offerings, and after a few such rounds, you don't much care, anyway—at least, not until the next morning.

Synthetic sake, which was developed during the Pacific War, still accounts for about one-tenth of all the sake consumed. *Mamushizake* (the *mamushi* is Japan's only poisonous snake) is sake in which this serpent has been embalmed and is taken as a restorative. In Hawaii, one can buy carbonated sake, which is faintly—but only faintly—reminiscent of dry champagne.

The Japanese drink 4.2 gallons of sake per person every year, while Americans drink just under $1\frac{1}{2}$ gallons of distilled spirits. (Criers of doom who are forever telling us that Americans are drinking more and more should note these comparisons: In 1960, the average per capita consumption of distilled spirits in the U.S. was 1.2 gallons. One hundred years before that, in 1860, the figure was 3.3 gallons, nearly three times as much.)

To draw a conclusion, however, from such a comparison

of sake and whiskey consumption would be meaningless. If we calculate the alcohol actually contained in various drinks, our intake is about twice that of the Japanese.

While the Japanese are consuming more beer and foreign-style liquors these days, sake is still the drink of choice when it comes to doing something of more significance than merely getting swacked. The *san-san-ku do* (three-three-nine times) sake drinking ritual is the high point of the Shinto marriage ceremony. Funerals are performed with sake. Births are celebrated. Ships are launched. New homes and buildings are blessed. Seasons are welcomed: All to the accompaniment of infusions of what the Japanese call the "Gift of the Gods."

Japanese-style dinners are begun with draughts of sake. Even if the guest doesn't like rice-wine or if he really has his eye on that bottle of Chivas Regal Scotch the serving wench has just brought into the room, it is better to at least take a sip of the contents of the *sakazuki* he will be offered. Otherwise, the host will murmur words of distress. (At lunches or dinners in Western-style surroundings, the toasts can be made in beer or whiskey.)

Shōchū, the drink referred to above, is written with characters meaning "the strong drink that burns." Its alcoholic content varies from 45 to 60 percent, and it is distilled from the dregs of sake or from sweet potatoes. Kagoshima, Kyushu's southernmost prefecture, has 141 distilleries that produce four and a half million gallons of this drink yearly, which is also known as "Satsuma vodka," Satsuma being the old feudal name of that region.

Even a production of four and a half million gallons, however, is not sufficient to slake the thirst of Kagoshima Prefecture's 1,900,000 inhabitants, who have to import half a million more gallons of *shōchū* from other prefectures. Even sober, Japan's southerners are known for their volatility and ebullience, and when spurred on by these ardent spirits, they rack up impressive records in crimes and accidents. In one recent year alone, for example, Kagoshima police reported no less than 112 incidents in which Japanese drunk on *shōchū* went to sleep on train tracks or in streets and were run over and killed.

As might be expected, the problem of drunkenness in Japan is different from that in the U.S. in several aspects. For one thing, there are not nearly as many genuine alcoholics in Japan, excepting the prefecture of Kagoshima mentioned above. Alcohol inebriates the Japanese more quickly because of their lesser consumption of animal fats and flesh and because of the binding behavioral restrictions of their society, which produces a compensating need for release. Given lesser actual consumption of alcohol and faster reactions to it, their bodies seldom reach the point where they require continuing infusions of spirits. Many Japanese react so quickly to alcohol that only two swallows of a martini will cause a speedy dilation of the capillary veins and a resulting feverishly red coloration of the skin. This reaction is so severe that many refuse to drink at all because of it.

In recent years Japanese professors Harada and Mizoi studied the livers of 60 Germans and 40 Japanese and found that those of their countrymen did not have a certain enzyme that breaks down acetaldehyde in the blood. It is the chemical acetaldehyde, they state, that reddens the face and leads to disorderly behavior.

Another differing aspect is that the Japanese have always been notoriously lenient and forgiving toward the inebriated ones, who can curse, cry, dance, cackle, sing, fight, and talk dirty without much fear of punishment or even a mild scolding.

Note what the Japanese themselves say about their country being a "drunkards' paradise":

". . . The first step toward the extermination of this nuisance is to train the public to believe that irresponsible conduct by drunkards must not be tolerated." (Mr.

Kondo, Chief of the Crime Prevention Department of the Tokyo Metropolitan Police Department.)

". . . the ordinary Japanese believes that the best policy is to endure everything and do nothing when the other party is drunk." *(Mainichi Daily News.)*

"In Japan, the drunkard's Eden, you may drink like a baboon and not lose an iota of respectability in the eyes of the people, be you a Lord Abbot or a Minister of Education." (Santaro's column in the *Asahi Evening News.*)

"Japan is a paradise for drunken men. Intoxicated behavior is dismissed lightly, even in criminal cases." (Mrs. T. Tazaki, vice-president of the Tokyo Federation of Women's Organizations.)

"In Japan there is a strange convention by which ordinary human beings strip themselves of their dignity when they drink, exposing their weaknesses and baring their hearts, confessing the most embarrassing secrets. No matter how they grumble or whine, they are completely forgiven on the excuse they have been drinking." (Yukio Mishima, novelist and playwright.)

Pfc. Adolph W. Merten, an American marine, was acquitted and released by a Japanese court after he had shot to death nineteen-year-old Shiro Takawa in a bar in Yokosuka. The Japanese judge explained that Merten had been drinking and so was non compos mentis at the time of the killing. (Clause No. 39 of the Penal Code reads, "Acts committed while of unsound mind shall not be punished," and drunkenness is equated with temporary mental imcompetence.)

That Merten's case is not so unusual is supported by this comment from the *Vox Populi, Vox Dei* column of the *Asahi Shimbun:* "There have been many cases in the past of murderers being acquitted or getting off with incredibly light sentences on the grounds that they were drunk and non compos mentis at the time of the crime.

One judge has been moved to complain with a heavy sigh, 'Japan is a paradise for drunkards.'"

To try to correct this situation, however, by legislating more severe penalties for public inebriation may result in serious trouble in other quarters. As suggested earlier, drunkenness is a major safety valve on the pressure chamber of the society. Clamping it shut could cause the excess pressure to seek release through even less desirable avenues.

Tremendous pressures build up internally and characterize Japan's social structure; any student failing to take them into account will not succeed in understanding the Japanese and their culture. In their vertical social arrangement, few are equal, and the Japanese spend much of their days calculating how much higher or lower they stand than the next fellow. And these precise distances govern the degree of respect or disrespect, the depth of the bow, the kind of language, the frequency of the smile, the willingness to oblige, and the extent of compliance that one Japanese must extend and show to another. The gauging of these distances and reactions alone is a time-consuming and often frustrating job. The denegation of individuality and the repression of personal choice in which they result would be stultifying to anyone, even people born in such surroundings and aware of no other system.

Sometimes individual Japanese can endure it no longer. A trigger will release their pent-up resentment, anger, and frustration, and explosions of varying intensity follow. Until now, drunkenness, quickly achieved and publicly flaunted, has been the major channel through which these explosive emotions have spent themselves. Of course, not everyone takes advantage of this form of release, which at least partially accounts for some other excessive behaviorism (suicides, riots, and crimes of violence) in Japan. Realizing this, the Japanese have tended to be lenient, if not sympathetic, toward men in their cups. Since it was a condoned activity, many Japanese came to take advantage of its pressure-reducing benefits. Indeed, things came to such a pass that failure to get looped when the opportunity presented itself was viewed with suspicion and distaste.

Santaro, the *Asahi Evening News* columnist mentioned above, wrote in one of his columns: "If a respected foreigner in this country wishes to gain the good opinion of his Japanese friends, he could do no better than to be their guest—or victim—at a Japanese dinner and get as drunk as a lord so that he had to be shoved into his car and taken home and have to tell his host on the morrow that he remembered nothing of the evening before. *It would elevate his credit in their eyes as nothing else could.*" (Italics mine.)

So commendable has inebriation become at most parties that some Japanese will pretend to be half-seas over when in reality they have had only a very small quantity of liquor. I was drinking on the Ginza with a Japanese friend one night when he received momentous news of changes in regulations that would permit his company to import a certain locally-scarce raw material in unlimited quantities. He happened to know that the president of his company was compoting that same evening in a restaurant in Shimbashi, so he and I hurried over there by taxi. A maid escorted us to the door of the large tatami room where an uninhibited bacchanalia was in full swing. My friend at last caught the eye of his company's president, who was down on all fours with his shirttail out, letting a geisha ride him around the room like a horse. In the few seconds it took him to get to his feet and reach us at the door, he had recovered much of his equanimity, and by the time he heard my friend report the news, he was stone-cold sober. Without hesitation, he issued comprehensive instructions covering quantities, shippers, dates, and terms of payment in fine detail and told my companion to cable the orders that same night.

We then watched him as he returned to the party. Before

he got half-way to his geisha's side, he had already begun to stagger again and as we were closing the door, he was getting down on his hands and knees, urging the geisha to mount him once more in an unsteady voice.

The Japanese were first exposed to the American and European disapproval of getting falling-down drunk at formal social gatherings with the influx of foreign teachers and advisers in the 1870's. Thereafter some Japanese attempted to restrain their alcoholic exuberance in the presence of foreigners, but most of them dismissed such niceties with contempt. They called it "killing the sake" (*sake wo korosu koto*).

By the middle of the 1970s, traffic accidents related to drunken driving had increased to the point where remedial action was required. As always, when the Japanese sense there is supportive concensus, they act quickly and decisively. In December, 1977, the Tokyo police, using a newly-developed breathalizer, started testing the amount of alcohol consumed by drivers. The law permitted no more than 0.25 milligrams of alcohol per liter of breath, which amount can be produced by only one drink.

The police developed a point system, whereby they noted nine points on the back of the driver's license for *any* trace of alcohol on the breath. When the score reached 15, the driver lost his license for one year. Even then it was not returned to him automatically. He had to take the onerous driving examination again.

The gendarmes became so strict that they even added points to the license of the bartender who served the customer drinks, if he knew that person would be driving.

In the first two years, arrests for drunken driving in Tokyo fell from 35,000 to 14,000.

Every year the Japanese increase their consumption of foreign-style hard liquors, both imported and distilled at home. Among the imported spirits, Scotch and gin are favorites, with little attention yet being given to American

Bourbon. The domestically-produced liquors cover a wide range of variety and quality, including one lavender-colored concoction bottled in a glass replica of Tokyo Tower that may have no equivalent in foreign lands. (At least, I hope not.) Imported spirits can be painfully expensive, with the exception of gin, which falls into a different classification for customs purposes, and so is more reasonable in price.

Foreign-style liquors have had a hard time getting off the ground in Japan, although Japanese living in Tokyo, Yokohama, and Kobe were exposed to them a hundred and more years ago. In one famous case, a liquor salesman tried to sell foreign whiskey to a kimono dealer in Hiroshima and ended up being arrested and charged with vending poison without a pharmaceutical license.

Suntory Ltd.—Japan's oldest and largest producer of foreign-style liquors (Suntory, Torys, Hermes, etc.)—tried to overcome public indifference in 1922 with a poster showing a "half-nude girl" drinking its Akadama Port Wine. Although the picture would be considered tame by today's standards, it created a scandalous sensation in the Japan of the 1920s. As a result, Suntory was swamped with orders for—not the wine—but copies of the poster. (Most Japanese wine is sweet and is still considered more a tonic than a pleasure-producing potation. It was once sold only in pharmacies.)

A team of Japanese distillation experts has been hard at work for some years now trying to develop the techniques needed to produce high-quality Scotch-type liquor in Japan. Considering the success the Japanese have had in producing the "three B's" (beer, bread, and beef, none of which were consumed in Japan until after 1853), it would not be at all surprising if they succeed admirably.

My first encounter with Japanese beer took place in Fukuoka, where I and five comrades-in-arms (all up-and-coming womanizers and profligates like myself) had arrived late one night to report for duty with our new military outfit.

Early the next morning we made our bleary-eyed way from the Ueno Ryokan, an inn destined to be the scene of many a whing-ding, to a nearby, seedy-looking building called the New Otani, our unit's mess-hall.

Our breakfast that morning was to be our first in the outback, so to speak, and we approached the table, beside which a smiling Japanese waitress stood bowing, with mixed feelings of caution and anticipation.

In the middle of the table stood three large brown bottles. Although without labels, the beads of moisture forming on their sides hinted of their contents. With alacrity surprising for that hour of the morning, we filled our glasses and drank . . . and then filled them again. We looked at each other . . . and nodded. It was unquestionably beer. *Good* beer.

When we had drained the three bottles, the still-smiling waitress (whom we logically named "Happy-san") fetched three more, whereupon we asked her to what special occasion we owed the lovely presence of beer on our breakfast table. She bowed again, then explained in her Hakata dialect it was the enlightened custom of the New Otani Mess Hall to serve free beer with *all* meals. Seeing our pleasantly surprised reaction to this she added that she had assumed *all* Americans drank beer with *every meal.*

We felt it was our duty not to disillusion her.

It might well be that, in the 16th and 17th centuries, Dutch and English merchants made home brew in their small, isolated trading posts on the islands of Dejima and Hirado off Kyushu, but the first factual account of beer being drunk in Japan concerns that offered by Commodore Perry himself to the officials of the tottering Tokugawa shogunate. (This was our first attempt at carrot-and-stick diplomacy and Perry's approach to cracking Japan's wall of self-imposed isolation: Offer them beer with one hand while using the other to point rather casually in the general direction of the big guns on his fleet anchored in the bay behind him.)

Not long after that a certain Dr. Kawamoto, who had studied Western medicine—and brewing techniques—from imported *Ban-sho* (barbarian books), is said to have constructed a vat in the garden of his residence in the Shimbashi district of Tokyo, but the good doctor and his jovial *nomi-nakama* (drinking buddies) must have consumed the entire output, for there is no record of any effort to market Kawamoto's Blue Ribbon Pilsener or any similarly named beer.

The first commercial-scale brewery was established in 1869 in Amanuma by a William Copland, a Norwegian by birth who became a naturalized U.S. citizen. Copland, who lies buried in Yokohama's cemetery for foreigners, should really have the inscription "Father of Japanese Beer" engraved on his tombstone, for the company he founded, the Spring Valley Brewery, Ltd., eventually grew to be the giant Kirin Brewery of today, one of the world's largest producers of beer.

Since Copland's early Amanuma Beer, some 126 brands have tried to capture the loyalties of Japan's beer-drinkers, but the competition in recent years has narrowed the field down to Sapporo, Asahi (called "Ash Eye" by the Australians), Ebisu, Suntory, and, of course, Kirin. (A *"kirin"* is the mythical flying, horse-like dragon seen on the label of this beer.)

As might be expected, one of those 126 brands was "Fuji," and the label on this beer read, "The efficacy of this Beer is to give the health and especially the strength for Stomach. The flavor is so sweet and simple that not injure for much drink."

For my money, all those now on the market are good, especially in draft on a hot summer afternoon, but Kirin has taken most of the market, followed by Sapporo and

Asahi in that order. In a recent poll, an American magazine rated Kirin as one of the world's very best—a conclusion with which such food-and-drink authorities as the famous Maurice C. Dreicer of New York finds no fault.

In volume consumed, beer has long since passed sake, making it, in that sense at least, the national drink of the Japanese.

Japanese beer comes in draft, two sizes of bottles, and pull-tab cans like those in the U.S., but one notable distinction between our breweries and theirs is that the Japanese have their own directly operated *biyā-hōru* (beerhalls). Many of these are situated atop downtown buildings for the summer season and feature colorful borders of paper lanterns, very audible Hawaiian bands and an occasional fountain, perhaps intended to stimulate the flow of suds.

Someday, when I'm rich and idle, it would be a pleasant diversion to lease a helicopter, stock it with a six-pack of Kirin, and hover low over downtown Tokyo early some summer evening to complacently regard what must appear from above to be a vast, eyeboggling expanse of rooftop beer gardens, a-dance with music and colored lights and droves of serving girls trotting among the crowded tables while carrying trays heavy laden with foaming schooners, beakers, and steins.

Even if you don't have a helicopter at your disposal, however, it is easy enough to locate one of the multitude of large beer halls scattered throughout Japan. Just head for any city's entertainment district—and look up. Wherever you see colored lanterns festooned around a roof area, that's probably a beer garden, either one of those operated by a big brewery chain, or an independent.

Some of these beer halls go to elaborate lengths to attract customers. Some feature go-go and rock music, others western or German beer-drinking songs, and lots of Hawaiian music, for which the Japanese seem to have an unaccountable affection.

One beer hall (the Ginza Lion) has a large collection of beer steins from all over the world, including some of solid gold, from which customers can quaff their suds—after putting up a cash deposit.

One of the beer hall chains even issues its own credit card for drinkers who prefer to drink on the cuff.

Somebody else might have invented beer, but nobody is more enthusiastic than the Japanese about the brew and the good times that go with it.

My introduction to Japanese tea drinking was instructive—and very filling. It came just after the war in Fukuoka, when I became the Liaison Officer for the Civil Censorship Detachment and was meeting the various Japanese officials, companies, and individuals with whom I would be doing business. Since we were to censor everything from stage plays to radio broadcasts, from personal letters to newspapers, it took more than a week for me to see all these people in the city of Fukuoka only, to say nothing of the island of Kyushu, and I had at least one cup of tea with each. I estimate the total consumption for the first week at 75 cups. Fortunately for me, the cups were small, and the Japanese consider it impolite to fill a teacup more than two-thirds full.

Even more than sake, tea is vital to the Japanese way of life and must be ranked after rice in importance. (Witness the Japanese expression for an everyday happening: *nichijō sahanji* or "a usual tea-and-rice thing.")

Tea first appears in Japanese historical records in the year of A.D. 729, when the Emperor Shomu invited one hundred Buddhist monks to join him for tea. This Imperial supply, however, may have been imported from China, because the first tea shrubs were reportedly grown from seeds brought back from China in 805 by a monk named Saicho.

Buddhist monks were the first to make significant use of tea, because it helped to keep them awake during long motionless hours of contemplation. They in turn recommended it for its medicinal properties to the Imperial court. For centuries thereafter tea was the drink of the aristocrats, samurai, and religious classes, and it was not until 1737, when a man named Nagatani of the Yamashiro district, near Kyoto, succeeded in making an unfermented tea called *sencha*, that the popularization of tea among all classes began. The life span of the Japanese did increase enormously after the introduction of tea but not because of the properties with which the priests endowed it. Rather, the people were living longer because they boiled the water with which they made their tea.

The Japanese word for tea is *cha* or, with the honorific prefix, *ocha*, while in Mandarin Chinese it is pronounced *ch'a*. As early as 1696, the the British were using the Chinese word for tea, and even today it is common to hear British workmen talk about a "cup of *char*." And in Russian the word for teahouse is *chaihana*, while in Persian it is *chaikhaneh*. In Swahili tea is called *chai*.

The best tea comes from Uji, near Kyoto,while the most comes from Shizuoka (50 percent), but production is by no means limited to these areas. The tea shrubs are grown mostly on terraces but many can be raised on level ground as well, if it is well-drained. The first harvest comes when the shrub is three years old, but the shrub produces its best tea between its fifth and ninth years. The infinite variety of tea comes not only from the location,kind, and age of the shrub but also from the time of the harvest, the location of the leaf on the branch, and, of course, the method of preparation.

Only one percent of Japan's annual tea production (totalling 80,000 tons) is black *(kōcha)*, while the rest is green. The Japanese drink black tea as we do, with combinations of sugar, lemon, and milk, but green tea is always taken without any additives. Whereas Americans average 7/10 of a pound of tea yearly (much of which is wasted in tea-bag form), Japanese consumption is nearly two pounds. If two pounds a year does not sound like much tea drinking, you should consider that a pinch of tea leaves will produce much more of this liquid refreshment than the equivalent weight, for example, of coffee.

The genuine tea-house *(chaya)* is fast disappearing from the Japanese scene. In *Things Japanese* Basil Hall Chamberlain wrote, "The tea-house is a thing by itself—in the country, an open shed, in the towns, often a pretty, but always open, house, sometimes with a garden, where people sit down and rest for a short time, and are served with tea and light refreshments only. . ."

In place of the tea-houses, we now find in towns *kissaten* (tea and coffee shops), where music may be the most important offering, and in rural areas *o-zashiki* (Japanese-style restaurants), where tea is assuredly served but is not the focal point of the guest's visit, which may be food, carousing, or dalliance.

When I was living in Tantakabayashi near Kobe, my landlord was in the habit of inviting me to his home next-door to the tea ceremonies *(chanoyu)* he held every Saturday afternoon. Because he was the retired president of a large steel manufacturing company, his other guests were often men of equivalent prominence, so I usually accepted his invitations for the opportunity they presented to exchange views with Japanese of distinction, although I had little real interest in the ceremony itself, which is surely one of the most esoteric aspects of Japanese culture.

Little by little—by a process of sheer osmosis, I suppose—I developed a tolerance, if not fondness, for the ceremony which was first codified by the Buddhist abbot Eisai and later more rigidly by Sen-no-Rikyu, whose descendents still operate one of Japan's best-known schools of the tea cult.

The origin of the tea-ceremony as we know it today is to be found in gatherings of Buddhist monks in front of an image of Bodhidharma to drink tea from a single bowl with all the formality of a holy sacrament. After this religious stage, the tea-ceremony moved on to a second sybaritic stage, in which the guests and host reclined, like ancient Romans, on fine furs and studied costly finery and works of art. Guests were invited to participate in such games as guessing where the tea being served was raised or where the tea-cups were made. For correct guesses, they were given the right to take their choice of any of the gold and silver vessels or brocades or swords arrayed before them. And it was the custom for these guests to pass on their prizes to the serving girls in attendance.

It was during this stage, in 1587, that the de facto ruler of Japan, Hideyoshi, gave what is most likely the largest tea-party ever held. Hideyoshi invited every devotee of the tea-ceremony in all of Japan to attend and warned that any who failed to come would be barred from ever participating in the ceremony again. The party was held in Kitano, near Kyoto, and lasted ten days. Estimates of the number of attendees range as high as 16,000.

One of the men who attended this party, the same Sen-no-Rikyu mentioned earlier, is the person most responsible for introducing the third and present stage of the tea-ceremony, in which stark simplicity is the keynote. Exhausted as their country was from long years of internal warfare, the life of the average Japanese had become increasingly difficult. The utmost frugality and plainness were in order. Reflecting the needs of the country, Sen-no-Rikyu took simplicity and restraint as his themes and around them built the tea-ceremony as we know it: "a worship of simplicity and of antique objects of art, together with the observance of an elaborate code of etiquette." He aimed at making it a cult of aestheticism and discipline designed to promote mental composure, internal peace, and enlightenment. Through it, he taught his disciples to be keenly aware, to sharpen their senses to discover depths of beauty that might not otherwise be apparent.

A typical tea-ceremony lasts two or three hours and is attended by the host or a tea-master, who may or may not be the same person, his assistant, and five guests. It is held in a small, separate building in the garden. Although the English translation is the same (tea house), this building is called a *sukiya* in Japanese and is different from the larger commercial tea-house mentioned earlier. The entrance through which one enters is small and cramped, which is designed to inculcate humility. Once inside, there is a set order in which the guests examine and praise the seemingly plain implements of the ceremony and other decorative objects. Some of the tea-cups, which to the untutored may look like unglazed, chipped rejects from a cheap porcelain factory, are often worth hundreds of dollars, if not more.

I found a cracked tea-cup at one of the first tea-ceremonies I attended and lost no time in pointing the crack out to the host, thinking that he did not know about it and that he would not want to expose his guests to possible injury from swallowing a chip or sliver of porcelain. He and his other guests smiled to cover their embarrassment, but later, when we were alone, my host explained to me that the misshapen, cracked, crudely colored tea-cup had been made that way two hundred years before. Seeing my amazement, he went on to point out that the forms of nature are always imperfect, that nothing in nature is symmetrical, and that the tea-ceremony, held as it is in the garden and at appropriate seasons of the year, is a reflection of nature; that a perfectly shaped, perfectly painted tea-cup would be entirely out of place. (Evidently this principle does not, however, apply to *all* the implements of the ceremony.)

The tea served at this ceremony *(matcha)* is made from a light-green powder mixed with hot water and swished around in the bottom of the cup with a *chasen* or bamboo tea-whisk. Each guest takes three sips of this bitter, foamy mixture and follows an elaborate ritual of when to bow, when to praise the quality of the tea, how to hold the cup, how to pass it on to the next guest, and so forth. It is a geometric progression in manners.

Although the guests may talk, the emphasis is on contemplative quietness and peace and the achievement of a silent symphony of graceful but restrained motion.

Today more than two million Japanese consider themselves full-fledged devotees of the tea-ceremony, about which Kakuzo Okakura wrote in his BOOK OF TEA: "Teaism is a cult founded on the adoration of the beautiful among the sordid facts of everyday existence. It inculcates purity and harmony.... It is essentially a worship of the imperfect. . . it is a religion of the art of life. . . (where) the host and guest join to produce for that occasion the utmost beatitude of the mundane. The tea-room is an oasis in the dreary waste of existence. . . . The ceremony is an improvised drama whose plot is woven about the tea, the flowers, and the paintings. Not a color to disturb the tone of the room, not a sound to mar the rhythm of things, not a gesture to obtrude on the harmony, not a word to break the unity of the surroundings, all movements to be performed simply and naturally—such are the aims of the tea ceremony."

It should be borne in mind that the tea ceremony was developed under the tutelage of Zen Buddhist priests, and its aim was to purify one's soul through unity with nature. Such words as 'calm,' 'grace,' and 'rustic country surroundings' typify the ceremony, whose heart may be best described by the phrase, "the aestheticism of austere simplicity and refined poverty," and by the selfless manner in which the host serves tea to his guests.

Matters Sexual

A frank sexuality permeates the atmosphere of Japan and soon becomes apparent to foreigners, especially those from countries only recently emerging from under the pall of Victorian precept. Some regard this sexuality as shocking, others find it charming, ambrosial, and stimulating. It may be the most forcible of the several reasons why many Americans have elected to become long-term residents of that country.

This is not, however, tantamount to saying that the Japanese are obsessed with sex. It is rather that they are more candid and realistic about it. To them, sex does not carry the stigma of evil, since it is not related to the question of morality. While they do not engage in it on the streets, they see no reason to smother or stunt it under a blanket of shame or to talk about it only in prurient whispers. Like all other spheres of Japanese activity, they assign it a place and surround it with rules, but within these prescribed boundaries they pursue it with vigor and indulge in it with gusto.

According to the quasi-historical Japanese legends about the creation of the universe, their gods lost no time in discovering sex, as in this version:

"Now Izanagi (the male deity) turned to the left and Izanami (the female deity) turned to the right and they circled the pillar of land separately. When they met on the far side, Izanagi said, 'How delightful! I have met a lovely maiden!'

"Then he asked Izanami, 'In thy body is there anything formed?' She answered, 'In my body, there is a place which is the source of femininity.' The male deity said, 'In my body there is a place which is the source of masculinity. I wish to unite this source-place of my body with the source-place of thy body.' "

What could be plainer than that? No mumbo-jumbo about serpents and apples and ribs and loss of innocence. Just a straight-forward, gentlemanly proposition, which was accepted in turn with fetching frankness and amenable anticipation.

Given this example set them by the first two deities in their Shinto pantheon, the Japanese went on during the subsequent centuries to seek uninhibited sexual gratification as often as they physically and financially could. And today, despite such setbacks as the Anti-Prostitution Law cf 1958, more Japanese are probably able to enjoy the benefits of a full sex life than ever before because of increased economic capability, greater freedom of choice and self-expression for women, less government-imposed social regimentation, and vastly enhanced opportunities for male-female communion.

Miss Kazuko Shiraishi, who is renowned as the *Dankon wo utau shijin* (poetess who extols the phallus), may not yet be typical of Japan's post-war emancipated women, but she is blazing a broad trail for others to follow in her bold march toward complete sexual freedom. Two of her more famous dicta are "*Boi-furendo wa nete kara erabe!*" (Choose your boy-friends only *after* you have tried sleeping with them!) and "*Kokujin no sekkusu wa saikō ne*" (Negroes do it best).

Increasingly women are bringing their sexual affairs, questions, and problems (mostly, it seems, of a quantitative nature) out into the open, which is not, however, to suggest that they were so well concealed in the past. Magazines that in the U.S. would be named *Seventeen* or *Debutante* or *Young Bride* print a continuing stream of articles and surveys about sex and the young girl. Although often written in a lurid style, much of the advice appears to be sound or, at least, non-toxic.

I have one such article before me now. It concerns a round-table discussion among five Tokyo girls, ranging in age from fourteen to nineteen, about female masturbation. The tone is serious, and the girls discuss the subject frankly. When did they first masturbate? What was the stimulus? Do they believe it is harmful? Do their boy-friends, if any, know about it? And so forth.

Articles and surveys about virginity are also numerous. Often they use the round-table discussion technique and probe in depth such questions as the age at which the girls lost their virginity, the place, the amount of pain or bleeding, and the identity of their partners. Among the categories of partners given in one set of answers I found one intriguing group called "old family friends."

Although one survey found that more than sixty percent of the girls questioned agreed, generally speaking, that a bride equipped with an intact hymen on her wedding night was somewhat better off than one without, the Japanese do not otherwise appear to attach to this condition quite the same abstract, absolute value that we do—or, at least, did until the onslaught of the Sexual Revolution that began in the Sixties.

An unbroken hymen certifies that its owner has not had sexual intercourse of the full-entry variety, and I suppose that no Japanese bridegroom would be too put out if he finds the one he has contracted to use permanently to be undamaged.

A ruptured hymen is, to us, an indication of loose behavior, but the Japanese fight shy of making such absolute judgments. Virgin or non-virgin does not necessarily equate to good or bad. Everything, they feel, must be considered against a background of relevant circumstances.

Why, they would want to know, did the girl in question

relinquish her chastity? Perhaps her seductor urged her to drink o-sake, to which she was not accustomed, in such quantity that she lost control of herself? Or could it be that he was a highly respected man to whom her entire family was beholden, and that her refusal to accommodate his sex urge would have disturbed the harmony of the relationship? Nothing, they would say, should be plucked from out of its proper surroundings and judged on the unsympathetic scales of cold Western logic. Many mitigating circumstances would justify the voluntary relinquishment of virginity, so many that it would be bootless to make much of an issue of the matter to begin with.

Post-marital chastity, however, is viewed in a somewhat different light, because the husband's face and the family reputation come into question. If a wife could gratify her sexual whims with no risk of bringing shame or discord to the family unit, she might very well do so, especially if her spouse has been derelict in his nocturnal duty. But the times in her life when she will have such unfettered opportunities may be fewer than those afforded her American counterpart.

The following letter which appeared in the Advice to the Troubled Column of a weekly magazine called *Shūkan Manga Sandei* illustrates the conflict between this concern for external appearances and sexual freedom for women. Signed by an Osaka woman who gave her name only as Shigeko, the first part of this lengthy letter relates that she is twenty-seven years old and that she has been married for three years and that her husband, who vouchsafes her his sexual favors only about once a month, is often away on business trips. The trouble begins when a twenty-three-year-old salesman of stocks and bonds begins to call at the house when the husband is out of town. Soon the wife and the salesman become lovers. Let's have Shigeko tell the rest of the story in her own words:

". . . . I had him come to the house often while my husband was away on trips and abandoned myself to violent sexual love with him. One day, however, my husband returned unexpectedly to find us naked together on the sofa in the living room, in flagrante delicto. Although my husband stood in the doorway glaring at us, my climax was approaching and I could not possibly stop, no matter what he did. Later, the three of us sat down and talked it over. My husband's first concern was whether or not the neighbors (we have no children or servants) suspected anything. When I convinced him that they did not have even the slightest suspicion, he said that he and I should continue to live together, that he did not want a divorce. My lover, however, insisted that if he could not marry me, he had to be able to continue to enjoy my body.

"At that we reached an impasse and now I must make this difficult decision. I love my husband spiritually and for that reason I do not want a divorce, but at the same time I do not wish to give up the wonderful physical experiences I have discovered with my lover. Please advise me what I should do."

The editor of the magazine column advised Shigeko to break off relations with her lover before the neighbors found out what was going on and, at the same time, to discuss the matter of her sexual requirements frankly with her husband.

Although the reason for it has now largely disappeared, the custom of giving *makura-e* to brides and sometimes bridegrooms was once very popular in Japan. *Makura-e* are wedding charts or pillow pictures, the latter name being derived from the fact that these pictures were placed under the pillows of newly-weds on their wedding night as a kind of felicitous and informative surprise.

In the form of a scroll, the *makura-e* depicted for the presumably ignorant all the decent and indecent things that the honeymooners might conceivably do to and for each other on that and subsequent nights. Judging from candid accounts of sex life in days when the pillow-pictures were in greater vogue, however, I suspect that the purpose of the *makura-e* was not so much to inform as merely to serve as a check-list, lest one of the newly-weds overlook in his or her excitement, one or two of the forty-eight standard positions.

While the *makura-e* presented the fundamental, the finer points were often conveyed by fond mothers and aunts to brides or young nubile females. Brief hours before killing herself, Lady Nogi thoughtfully took time out to pen a lengthy, specific letter to her favorite niece telling her of the many things she should and should not do on her wedding night. One of the noble Lady's prime points of caution concerned the paper with which the bride was expected to wipe away the aftermath of the encounter. Extreme care should be taken, Lady Nogi stressed, not to let the paper crackle, for that could offend the sensitive ears of her consort, who would be relaxing in that delicate state of post-coital trance.

Many districts of Japan have their own endemic customs for celebrating the wedding night. The intent of some is to embarrass, of others to facilitate the pending carnal union. A rural district near Lake Yamanaka in the foothills of Mt. Fuji has a quaint custom that calls for the bride to jump over an open fire before entering her new home. Nowadays she does this fully clothed with the flames too low to touch her, but according to the original version of the custom she was expected to make the leap naked over flames that rose much higher. The purpose was to burn off any excessive pubic hair, which might otherwise interfere with the pending sexual activity.

Another rural usage—and one that is regrettably dying out—is called *yobai*, meaning "crawling at night." I first read about this in a book entitled *Suye-Mura: A Japanese Village*, by John Embree, an American scholar who spent a year in a small country town in Kyushu to learn the actual living conditions of the people. Later I came across other substantial verifications.

To understand this fine old custom, it is necessary to first realize that there may be a considerable number of people in the average Japanese farm-house: the farmer and his wife, their children, perhaps a widowed aunt, a maid (who works for little more than her board), an unmarried sister of the wife, a city cousin come to spend his summer vacation on the farm, among other visitors. Although the farmer may be poor, his home will expand to accommodate many tenants, each of whom requires only a *futon* (comforter) and a $3' \times 6'$ mat to sleep on. Among this welter, there may often be one or two unattached males or females who are not related by blood.

If, during the night, one of these males takes it into his head that he would like to share Mieko's or Shizue's or Tamayo's *futon* for a brief period, he ties a towel around most of his face and commences to crawl through the dark over the soft tatami matting toward the room where his intended true love happens to lie sleeping. Upon arrival, he nudges her into wakefulness and tries to crawl between the *futon* with her.

If she accepts him, love blooms. If she doesn't, he retreats to his lonely bachelor bedding. Being otherwise rejected would, of course, mean stultifying loss of face, but this is where the country gallant's towel comes into play. Because his face was concealed—because, in effect, he was supposedly unknown to her, he does not have to come to grips with this rejection and loss of face at all. He merely pretends that it did not happen. Now, he obviously knows who the woman was, and she knows very well who he was, but the towel around his head provides her with tenuous justification for pretending that she did not know. And since she doesn't know who he was, why should he lose face?

As elsewhere, the country folk in Japan are more down-to-earth in their attitude toward the natural functions of the body, although the city dwellers are not exactly backward in these matters, either. For some years after the end of the Pacific War, the Japanese authorities, prompted by our Occupation Forces, tried to persuade, by admonition and exhortation, the people to stop relieving themselves at the side of the road. They might as well have saved their breath. (I remember recently seeing a sign in a small plot of grass facing the busy thoroughfare between Roppongi and Iigura-machi in Tokyo that read in Japanese, "Do not defecate here.")

Fertility festivals are popular in the rural districts and are held yearly in such prefectures as Mie, Fukuoka, Kumamoto, Aichi, Wakayama, and Kagawa. Childless women entreat the God of Fertility to enable them to bear children, preferably sons. Such supplicants for divine benediction march in the festival parades carrying phallic symbols. These reproductions of the male organ are made of wood and vary in size from dildos of diffident dimensions through lengthier, lustier linga on to megalomaniacal delusions of grandeur.

The annual fertility festival in Kumamoto, near the town where John Embree uncovered *yobai* for the enlightenment of the Western world, has, I believe, the largest of these *jinzō inkei*, as the Japanese would call them. Cut from a log, it is thirty feet in length and two-and-a-half feet in diameter. Loaded on a wagon, it is pulled through the streets by a dozen or so frenetically envious young men.

OK alternative form of lingam.

Although they obviously could not carry such a monster as this, many childless women—calculating that the larger the phallic symbol, the greater the degree of ensuing divine intervention—can be seen staggering along behind the thirty-footer clasping to their breasts wooden replicas, some of which are five feet in length and eighteen inches in diameter. These are hollowed out from the base-end so that they will not be impossibly heavy.

When I once chanced to attend that festival in Kumamoto, I came across a tourist party of elderly American men and women who were waiting between trains and who had ventured forth from the railway station on their own to view the gala parade. Most of them had cameras and were avidly taking pictures of the childless female supplicants and their wooden "posts" as they passed. The Japanese, pleased to observe this foreign interest in their native culture, smiled and lifted their symbols in greeting. Some even stopped to let the foreigners—still unwitting, of course—touch and pat the wooden objects they were carrying. One Japanese woman, I remember, had tied a large green ribbon in a bow around hers, and the American tourists delayed her for several minutes while they admired and photographed it. At length one of the tourists sighted my American face and hurried over to ask me what the festival was all about, so that she could explain it to the neighbors back home when she showed them the movies she was taking. The others in the party followed her over and, encircling me, cut off my contemplated retreat.

Try as I would, I could think of no other plausible explanation to offer for the wooden do-funnies the Japanese women were carrying and so at last, I told them the plain truth.

When the full import of what I had said struck them, their reactions varied: Some blanched and left immediately for the train station, casting uneasy glances back over their shoulders. Others fell silent and began to sidle away from me. One woman straight away asked her husband how she could erase that part of the movie film without ruining the rest of the strip. Another opened her camera, removed the entire roll of film, and tossed it in the gutter in disgust. A third muttered something about leaving this heathen country for home the next day.

What with fertility festivals and forests of phallic symbols and night-crawling and pillow-pictures and sex drug stores and no-holds-barred discussions and illustrations of sex in a plethora of periodicals for young people, Japanese parents never need to tell their children about the birds and bees.

Perhaps the most effective way to set the mood for a brief discussion of prostitution in Japan is to look first at the two characters for the word *baishun*, which means prostitution: as with most Japanese ideographs, each of these has two readings: the first being read *bai* or *uru* and meaning to sell, and the second being read *shun* or *haru*, with the meaning of spring, in the seasonal sense. Hence, "to sell spring."

How much more friendly a term it is than "whoring" or "street-walking." (Consider also their word for red-light district: *karyūkai* or "flower and willow world.") The fearful disdain and anxious contempt with which we of the Western world view those women who deal in springtime are reflected in these and other harsh, bitter expressions we use to describe this business and its female merchandizers: bawdy house, cat house, stews, hooker, tart, doxy, slut, pig, hustler, tramp, chippy, and harlot. But the Japanese do not view it in this light, and a quick glimpse at the history of their licensed prostitution, which began in the year of 1193, may suggest why.

Japanese farming families have always welcomed the birth of sons more than daughters, for sons meant more hands to harvest the rice-paddies and garden-plots and to care for their parents in old age, while daughters were of more limited usefulness and, in addition, had to be supplied with dowries when they were taken in marriage. In times of poor crops and natural disasters the least useful members of the family unit, namely, the daughters, were sacrificed for the sake of familial survival. (The practice of *mabiki*—"weeding out" children, especially girl children, at birth—was common for hundreds of years and is evidenced in the Japanese proverb, *Ko wo suteru yabu ga aredo oya wo suteru yabu wa nai,* or "Although there is a bamboo grove where you can leave your babies to die, there is none where you can leave your parents.")

The daughters chosen to save their families were "sold" to brothel-owners, in whose establishments they were placed under long-term employment contracts and where it was difficult to ever get enough money ahead to redeem their freedom.

Japanese society recognized that these girls were innocent pawns in a struggle for survival. Their quiet acceptance of this fate, in fact, bespoke their willingness to abandon their personal dreams of having their own homes and families in order that their families might live. They were regarded with pity—and some respect.

The brothels in which these girls worked were mostly concentrated in regulated areas throughout the country, often surrounded by walls or moats, like Tobita in Osaka and Yoshiwara in Tokyo. The latter became the most famous in Japan, lasting from the early 1600's until its death by government decree on the first day of April, 1958. In its heyday, it was a city within a city, with high-class shops and all the sources of supply and service it needed to function as a municipal entity. Called the *Fuyajō* (the castle that knows no night), it closed its gates at midnight, which was the hour of curfew, but the revellers trapped within merely continued their bacchanalias until the gates were opened again at six o'clock the following morning. The prostitutes themselves could leave the environs of Yoshiwara for only two reasons: to visit dying parents or, in a group, to see the cherry blossoms in Ueno, which betokens the importance of cherry blossom viewing in the Japanese scheme of things. Samurai, otherwise not permitted to enter, went there in disguise and in droves, as did merchant princes and artists and poets and writers of stage plays. The leading prostitutes were idolized and glamorized to an extent reminiscent of the nimbus of awe in which American movie queens of the Thirties lived and thrived.

In the early 1600's, an Edo vice lord persuaded the authorities of the Tokugawa Shogunate to grant him a license to operate an area of supervised prostitution in exchange for surveillance on his part of suspicious strangers, about whom the ever-wary Tokugawas were always eager to obtain information. License in hand, he found an empty field grown up in reeds (Yoshiwara meant reedy field), and there his bagnio was born. Later a different character with the same reading—*Yoshi*—was substituted, and the meaning changed to happy field. After a fire in 1656, these quarters were moved to the Asakusa district of Edo, where they remained under the same name until their demise in 1958.

After this move, the quarters grew in glitter and gaiety, in size and sensuality, and in reputation and range of services and pleasures offered. As might be expected in Japan, everything was graded and classified and regulated. The main artery of Yoshiwara was a street lined with expensive shops, public baths, and fine restaurants, and the nearer this street the house of assignation stood, the higher its presumed quality.

The girls too were classified. When they first came to Yoshiwara (some as young as six or seven), they were called *kamuro* or apprentice-prostitutes. When they turned twelve, they were given examinations, and, if they passed, they were promoted to *shinzō* (written "newly-constructed") status and allowed to continue their studies in dancing, poetry composition, singing, and love-making—but the last by hearsay only. If they failed, they were consigned to perpetual maid status.

At the age of seventeen, the *shinzō* took examinations again, and those who passed this time entered the highest of the three major prostitute categories, that of *oiran*. Those who failed entered one of the two lower categories, *jijorō* or *sancha*, in accordance with their scores.

A census of the Yoshiwara for the year of 1689 certified the presence of 1,300 *jijorō*, 1,000 *sancha*, and just under 500 *oiran*. Again the *oiran* were sub-divided into three grades, the highest of which was called *tayū*. In the year just mentioned, there were only three *tayū* in all of Yoshiwara.

So elite were the *tayū* that they were not required to engage in the sex act with any man, and under no circumstances—not even if the *tayū* herself desired it—was a coupling permitted at their first meeting, for which it was mandatory that the suitor make an appointment well in advance. Since he was not permitted to enter her rooms, which were often lavishly decorated at ruinous cost to one or more of her lovers, the meeting took place at a *machiai* or assignation house elsewhere within the quarters. The *tayū* and her retinue of *kamuro, shinzō,* and *gyūtarō* (male servants)—looking like a festival or miniature parade—made this short journey on foot in the afternoon, the better to be admired and envied by all and sundry.

The purpose of this first meeting in the *machiai* was to provide the *tayū* with a chance to give her would-be lover the once-over. This she did while her *shinzō* entertained him with song and dance. If he found favor in her eyes, she would let him know, although indirectly: a gesture, a nod on parting. Or perhaps she would drop a hint in the title of a song she would instruct one of her *shinzō* to sing. Overwhelmed though he might be by this subtle accolade, our Lothario had to control his passions during a second meeting too, since it was not until the third rendezvous, if then, that this creme de la creme of Yoshiwara's Flower and Willow World would even entertain the notion of lowering herself to such a labor of love as one that would necessitate her becoming en rapport on the floor with this epitome of mere male impudence. And then only after certain understandings of considerable financial significance had been arrived at.

As Lord Chesterfield might well have observed, the cost of coition with a Yoshiwara courtesan, *tayū* grade, was damnable. Their wealthy patrons lavished every conceivable gift on them. One silk merchant "bought the time" of all the prostitutes in Yoshiwara for one entire evening to celebrate his arduous and at last successful courting of the reigning *tayū* of the time. Another, a rice dealer, bought all the eels in Edo one hot day in late July of 1724 so that the *tayū* who was—when she was not otherwise occupied—his true love would be the only woman in the Shogun's capital to dine on energy-restoring eel (a prime delicacy of the dog days) that summer night.

When they had spent their patron's money on everything else they fancied, the four or five (seldom more than six) *tayū* of the quarters entered into reckless kimono competitions with each other. At first they sought out the most attractive, then the most expensive kimono from the fanciest shops. Then they competed in quantity, until their rooms and even borrowed space would hold no more. Finally it reached the stage where the *tayū* was shamed if she wore any kimono, no matter how costly, more than once, while two and even three costume changes a day were sometimes in order.

With all that economic power available, one pauses to wonder why the *tayū* did not simply buy their way out of this enforced, albeit often sybaritic, servitude. Doubtless some did. There are stories to support this, but at that distance in history, it is hard to distinguish factual account from romantic legend.

Although Yoshiwara's slow descent from glory began as far back as 1760 (caused by changing social conditions and attitudes), the nadir was not reached until the date mentioned earlier: April of 1958. The rate of descent accelerated during the militaristic regime of the Thirties and early Forties, until it plunged to stagnation as the war neared its end.

The advent of our red-blooded American boys, however, staved off disaster, at least for a while. In fact, it acted like a pint of adrenalin pumped into the main artery. The prostitutes perked up and prospered as American sailors, marines, and soldiers strolled along the streets of Yoshiwara, gaily lit with lanterns and hope again, regarding and then selecting the merchandise on display.

On January 21, 1946, the office of the Supreme Commander, Allied Powers dispatched a memorandum to the Japanese government urging that it take steps to abolish legalized prostitution, including, of course, the Yoshiwara. This memo shocked Japanese solons. Abolish the gay quarters? What on earth for? What could possibly be wrong with it? What would take its place? They were so astounded and distressed that it took them one full year to respond and to make initial motions in the direction of compliance.

Having pressured Japan's lawmakers into accepting a new Constitution, the officials of the Occupation were then hesitant about forcing a sweeping anti-prostitution edict down their throats. They preferred to let the Japanese adopt the proposal and take the reins themselves.

The Japanese did just that. The Japanese women, that is. The newly-elected female members of the Diet called for the cooperation of women's organizations a-borning all over Japan in that early dawn of their emancipation and they made a strong fight of it. Interestingly enough, these women supported the abolition of licensed prostitution not so much from fear that their husbands might falter from the path of virtue and stumble into such lairs of temptation but more from concern over the fate of the prostitutes themselves. They held prostitution—and, in particular, enforced prostitution—to be the penultimate indignity a woman might suffer.

It took them eleven years, but at last they won. The quarters in Yoshiwara closed their gates to seekers of carnal pleasures and were converted in time to a district of coffee shops and restaurants, including one youth hostel. Although it became a crime for a woman to "sell spring," it did not become a crime for a man to buy it. In 1966, the women of Japan tried to correct this oversight; they sought the passage of a bill that would make it illegal for a man to buy the services of a prostitute or even to ask anyone to help him find such a woman. The fine would have been ¥10,000.

The bill was defeated, mostly because the male legislators of Japan were in no mood to consider any extension of the Anti-Prostitution Law. A curtailment would have been more to their liking. During those eight years since 1958, strains of syphilis resistant to the new drugs were appearing and proliferating alarmingly. Instead of being rehabilitated, most of the former dwellers of Yoshiwara and other quarters had reverted to their previous prone proclivities, in the guise of masseuses, girl guides, Turkish bath attendants, waitresses, cabaret hostesses, and models at nude-posing studios. Those who worked with pimps (who often doubled as gangsters) found themselves slaves to masters more heartless and demanding than any Yoshiwara brothel-keeper. Sex crimes, which had always been low in Japan, were growing in number, and this, suggested Justice Minister Okinoro Kaya, might be traced to the closure of the gay quarters.

No, indeed. The legislators might not yet have the ammunition they needed to justify reopening the quarters, but they most assuredly were not going to try to arrest and fine every man who asked someone the whereabouts of a whore. "Let's defeat this ridiculous proposal," they agreed. "After that, we'll bide our time for a while longer. Then we'll see."

Beyond any doubt, the one Great Saga of Sexual Love in modern Japanese times is that of Kichizo and Sada (or O-Sada, if you wish to prefix the honorific "O" to her first name).

Kichizo was Kichizo Ishida, who, with his wife, owned and managed an inn in Tokyo, where Miss Sada Abe, thirty-one, found empoyment as a maid one day in May. Within a week Kichizo and Sada had decided that they were meant for each other and set about proving it, but Mrs. Ishida quickly scented the danger and ran Sada out of the inn.

Sada retreated to the Masaki, a house of assignation in Arakawa Ward, where she entrenched herself, recouped, and estabished a line of communication with Kichizo. Forthwith, she ordered him to join her and to come prepared for a long siege.

Making the excuse of an urgent business trip, Kichizo left his wife and his inn and travelled across Tokyo to the Masaki in Arakawa. There he had his work cut out for him, but he settled down to it manfully. For six days and six nights, according to later testimony given by the maids of the Masaki, he and Sada locked themselves in a long, marathon-like embrace, breaking apart only long enough to snatch a short nap or a hurried snack. The maids were particularly distressed (some say envious) because at times the lovers would not leave off even when one of them entered the upstairs tatami room to bring the couple revitalizing sustenance.

On the eighteenth of May, at about eight in the morning, Sada came downstairs and told the maids that she was going out for a while and that they should let Mr. Ishida sleep as late as he liked.

At noon, however, Sada still had not returned, so one of the maids decided to ask Kichizo what she should bring him for lunch. A moment later, she came scrambling back down the stairs, screaming to the limits of her vocal power. Another maid summoned the police without even waiting for her co-worker to regain a semblance of sanity.

When they got there, the police found the Kichizo had been strangled with a woman's sash made of pink crepe, but what had sent the maid into orbit was the artwork that someone, presumably O-Sada, had decorated his corpse with.

On his left thigh, the ardent artist had written, in blood, four characters that read *Sada Kichi futari*, meaning "Sada and Kichizo, we two." On the left arm she had *carved* the single character for Sada. Then, from an apparently copious supply of blood, she had traced on the sheet in bold strokes five characters meaning "Sada and Kichizo, we two alone."

The primary source of all the blood? She had neatly amputated his male organ with a butcher knife.

Immediately O-Sada's crime captured the attention of the nation. Nor was it entirely unwelcome, for it contributed greatly to the alleviation of the oppressive tension that had been hanging over Japan like a miasma during the three months following the terrible assassinations and political turmoil of February 26, 1936. Perversely, the heinous mutilation of Kichizo Ishida—inspired, as it seemed to be, by intense passion of another sort—restored the country to a state of equanimity and tolerable good humor. The newspapers and tea-shops, the magazines and bars buzzed with excited talk of little else.

Three days later the ever-efficient Japanese police arrested Sada in an inn in Takanawa, on the road leading out of Tokyo south to Yokohama. The arresting officer, Detective Ando, found Kichizo's underwear and personal effects in one of Sada's bundles but not that one object without which Kichizo could not go to his grave a complete, if cold, corpse. Bluntly he asked her what she had done with it.

Shyly, Sada withdrew it, neatly wrapped in paper, from the bosom of her kimono where she had carried it since its amputation. Asked why she had taken it, she replied simply that it was the one thing that held for her the fondest memories.

Asked then why she had killed her lover, Sada answered that she could not abide the thought of any other woman having him.

Still, one of the interrogating detectives was dubious. How, he wanted to know, had a slight, willowy woman like Sada over-powered a man of Kichizo's stalwart physique? Sada explained that in their sexual experimentation she and Kichizo had discovered that if she applied pressure to his throat while in each other's arms and then suddenly released her grip, the resurgence of the temporarily obstructed blood through his veins dilated his phallic weapon, much to the enhancement of their mutual enjoyment.

At first I was doubtful about this phenomenon until I found corroboration in doctors' accounts of executions by hanging, which reportedly end in such tumescence.

During their six days of dalliance, Sada had done this to Kichizo so often that he evidently was not in the least alarmed when she wrapped her pink sash in lieu of her dainty hands around his neck and began to pull it tighter and tighter.

Imagine his surprise when she neglected to release it.

Charged with the crimes of murder and corpse mutilation, Sada was brought to trial. She was seemingly indifferent to her fate until she learned that she was also charged with sexual perversion. That really made her mad.

Murder? Yes, she was guilty of that. Mutilating a corpse? Yes, she had done that, too. But no one was going to call her a pervert and get away with it. So, for the first time, Sada took advantage of her right to have legal counsel, and with her lawyer, she began to fight to have this cruel accusation stricken from the list of charges. At length, the court called in expert psychiatric witnesses who testified, after examination, that Sada was not a *hentai-seiyokusha* (a sex pervert) but only an *ijō-seiyokusha*. (an oversexed person).

Gratified with this vindication, Sada smilingly admitted her guilt to the other charges and was given the extraordinarily mild sentence of only six years in prison.

One day not long after the close of the war in the Pacific, I was walking down the streets of Atami, hand in hand with an attractive Japanese maiden who had agreed to accompany me on my first trip to that resort town. We had arrived but a short while earlier and were taking a walk through town prior to retiring for the night. As we passed a certain inn, my companion told me—with an unsettling smile—that Miss Sada Abe worked therein.

I knew the story, of course, but I had no idea that Sada was working right there in Atami. All the grim details came flooding back. Nervously, I looked at Yoko (my companion) again and decided that I did not at all like the way she kept smiling at me. (I have since seen the same look come over the faces of other Japanese women when the name of Miss Sada Abe is mentioned.) Deciding that caution should be my watchword for the night, I returned to our room, pretended to telephone a number in Tokyo, and then announced that an emergency situation at my unit required that I return immediately.

Not long after that Miss Sada Abe left Atami. (Her presence may have had a similar disquieting effect on other male visitors; Atami, after all, is Japan's capital for "weekend honeymooners.")

Some years ago I read that she was working as a waitress in a small bar-and-restaurant in Asakusa in Tokyo, but I now believe that she is no longer in this vale of tears.

The trouble is that Sada's story has inspired too many other Japanese women to similar forms of revenge on men who are in the process of casting them aside for someone else. During the Occupation, one Japanese girl did something at least as colorful, if not so final and barbaric, to her American lover.

The American's wife was expected to arrive from the U.S. the next morning, so he had gone to pay his Japanese girl-friend one last visit the night before. The Japanese girl had protested and cried and begged, but he took refuge in whiskey and stubborn silence. It was very late when he finally went to sleep, fully clothed and stoned by alcohol, on the tatami.

When he began to snore, the girl made ready to wreak her vengeance. But instead of amputating it, as Sada had done, she merely painted it with red fingernail polish. (If not a manicure or a pedicure, then a phallicure?)

The next morning she deliberately let him sleep until the last minute, then awakened him brusquely and told him that he had only a few minutes to get out to Haneda to meet his wife's plane. Bleary-eyed and still only half awake, he splashed water on his face and staggered out of her room. When he got to Haneda, his wife was already there waiting for him, so he wasted no time putting her in his car and driving to the hotel where they would stay until permanent quarters could be assigned to them.

As he told the story to me a few weeks later, he was hung way, way over that morning and in no mood for romance but he realized that if he didn't pretend to be bursting with sexual desire, his stateside wife would, quite reasonably, want to know into what other avenues of release he had been channelling all that energy.

Summoning his wilted forces, he manfully escorted her forthwith to the bed in their hotel room and prepared to do the best he could under the circumstances. But as he disrobed, his wife instantly spied the splash of color—he later learned that the shade of the fingernail polish was "Flaming Glory"—with which he had been affectionately adorned.

Even more astounded than his wife, he was utterly unable to think of any explanation at all. Stunned, he could only slump down in a chair and stare in open disbelief.

His wife returned to the U.S. on the next available flight, and he and the Japanese girl were soon reunited.

Japanese Views of the West

Since the Japanese were an isolated, ethnically homogenous people for so long, it should not be too surprising that they developed rather strange national concepts of us Westerners, whom they called *gaijin* or people from the outside.

In the 18th century, a Dutch vessel berthed off Nagasaki in Kyushu. An extant diary of one of the Japanese visitors to the ship records his astonishment at the appearance of the crew: "When we boarded the ship, the captain and the crew removed their caps and greeted us. . . . They were men of pale and drab complexion with yellow hair and green eyes. It was hard to believe they belonged to the same world as ours. . . . They appeared to us to be devils or demons. Anyone, I am sure, who sees them would be scared and would run away. . . . "

Làter, when Commodore Matthew Perry and his Black Ships arrived off Uraga, Japanese artists swarmed aboard and furiously sketched everything in sight with swift brush strokes on mulberry-bark paper. With eerie uniformity of perception, all of the sixteen artists depicted the many Americans they drew as if they belonged to the same family. All had enormous, pointed noses, were covered with hair, and were huge. Our eyes were still green (later, they became blue), but now our hair was red instead of yellow.

Commodore Perry, who was actually clean-shaven, was shown as a slant-eyed demon, heavily bearded and mustached, with eyebrows as bristling as a steel-wire brush.

All that hair plus its redness must have impressed the

Japanese deeply for they prefixed their word for hair (*ke*) to one of their words for foreigners from China (*tōjin*) and named us *ketōjin* or hairy foreigners.

Shortened to *ketō*, this pejorative is still in use, but no more so, perhaps, than the equally offensive "Jap" is abroad. (It quite escapes me why Americans who can so blithely say "Jap"—as if it were altogether correct and proper—will not do other foreigners (including ex-enemies) the same courtesy and so say Hun for German, Frog for French, Wop for Italian, Spik for Spaniard, Kike for Israeli, Limey for Englishmen, Chink for Chinese, and Greaser for Mexican.)

And even though the percentage of red-heads among us is relatively small, the Japanese concocted another appellation for us, *kōmō gaijin* (lit., red-haired outsider), which is still considered standard Japanese.

In the many years that have passed since Perry first visited Japan, our physical image has not improved greatly in Japanese eyes. While granting that we are generally larger and stronger, the Japanese have grave misgivings about some of our habits of personal cleanliness. In the words of Ichiro Kawasaki, the candid and plain-spoken ex-diplomat who wrote *The Japanese Are Like That* and *Japan Unmasked*, "Westerners have a strong body odor that is quite nauseating." This smell, of which we are blissfully unaware, comes from our consumption of animal fat which produces butyric acid in our perspiration.

Back in the days when the Dutch traders were quarantined on the island of Dejima in Nagasaki Harbor, they were required to make an annual pilgrimage to the seat of the Shogun's government to make obeisance and offer gifts. A popular *haiku* of the time said of them,

When the Dutch	Oranda no tōjō ni
Come up to the capital,	Hae mo
Flies follow them.	Tsuite kite

Further, the Japanese regard our repeated discharge of

nasal mucous into the same piece of folded cloth as unspeakably filthy. Instead, they use and then discard thin sheets of paper. Because we wear our shoes indoors, they feel that our houses are no cleaner than public streets. By using disposable chopsticks in public eating places, they believe that they lessen the hazard of the contagion that might otherwise come from poorly washed utensils. When they have a cold, they often wear gauze masks, like those used by surgeons, over their nose and mouth to protect others from their germs. If they shake hands at all, they do so only with a noticeable lack of enthusiasm, for they shrink from such bodily contact.

They particularly question our toilet seats. (The Japanese toilet is an oblong basin set in tile over which the user squats. The position is tortured, but no exposed flesh comes into contact with anything touched by a previous user.) Office buildings in Japan's cities often provide both Western and Japanese-style toilet facilities. When a Japanese is forced to use the Western-style toilet, he will often squat over it with his shoes on the rim of the seat in preference to allowing his skin to come into contact with it.

If these are among the Japanese views of our physical characteristics, what then of our spiritual qualities? Do they think we are generous or miserly, kind or cruel, wise or foolish, forthright or devious, forgiving or vindictive? Do they genuinely like or despise us?

Obviously, the answers to such questions can be neither simple nor pat. Few Japanese wholly condemn or completely support us. Each has his own mixture of resentment and appreciation, of praise and censure, of superiority and inferiority convictions, all of which are subject to barometric changes brought on by international developments and Japanese interpretations of them and to geographic considerations. (The nearer the U.S. military base, the lower the regard in which we are held.)

This ambivalent attitude toward Westerners was formed, according to Dr. Hiroshi Minami of Hitotsubashi University in Tokyo—one of Japan's best-known psychologists, during the Meiji Era when his country began to import large numbers of Western teachers and experts to help Japan catch up with the Western world.

Most of the thousands of foreign scholars and specialists were highly respected by the Japanese. They brought with them not only their own expertise but also selected products from their own culture, also designed to impress the Japanese.

The wondrous Black Ships of Perry and the thousands of elite *gaijin* who poured into Japan during the two decades of the 1870's and 1880's made an almost unerasable imprint on the Japanese national mind. There was much, they decided, that was good about the West, and much to be learned or bought or copied from it.

But as their acquaintance with the world beyond the seas deepened, the Japanese could not help observing we too were formed from the common mold, with as many disfigurations as virtues. Their national self-esteem reasserted itself; the *gaijin* became, in their view, "people most remarkable like ourselves," as Kipling might have said it. We too had warts, or worse.

In the end, neither view truly ever replaced the other, except during armed hostilities. Both persisted, and often enough in the same mind.

To examine their opinions of us, we should first consider our views of them, since the two are interactive and reciprocal.

As a nation, we have gone through rather distinct stages in our kaleidoscopic and often unrealistic images of the people of Japan. From the "heathen Japanee" of pre-Perry days, we progressed to the giggling, shuffling Three Little Maids from School of Gilbert and Sullivan's *Mikado* and on to the quaint, colorful, unreal, toy-like Japanese of *Madame Butterfly*. Then Lafcadio Hearn gave us the Japan he saw through his uniquely tinted glasses—a charming, romantic, mystic country with a misty, other-world atmosphere. Later their immigration to our West Coast fixed in our consciousness a concept of the Japanese as a race of gardeners, valets, and truck farmers. When these immigrants began to compete economically and successfully with our own natives, we started to talk in worried tones about the Yellow Peril.

And all this while Western writers were turning out books whose very titles reflected our attitudes toward the Japanese: *Mysterious Japan, Behind the Japanese Mask, Unfathomed Japan, Behind the Smile in Real Japan, Japan's Islands of Mystery, Queer Things About Japan, Glimpses At Quaint Nippon*, and others.

Next came the Panay Incident ("So sorry, prease") and the Rape of Nanking, when we were told about Japanese soldiers who callously bayonetted Chinese babies. Our growing suspicions of the Thirties turned diamond-hard on the seventh of December in 1941, and after that our mental picture of the Japanese became the caricature we saw in "Slap the Jap" and similar war-time posters: a grinning, buck-toothed, bespectacled, crew-cut, bow-legged, monkey-like dwarf from whose pores dripped cunning, treachery, cruelty, arrogance, and brutality.

When the war had ended and some of our bitterness began to diminish, still another image of the Japanese took shape. Almost imperceptibly and indistinctly at first, a different kind of Japanese appeared on our mental screens. We had been surprised and pleased by the lack of resistance to our Occupation Forces. Loaded with samurai swords and bartered kimonos, our men in uniform returned from Occupation duty in Japan with favorable reports: The Japanese aren't so bad after all, they said. More than a few of our veterans even reenlisted in order to go back to Japan. Others brought Japanese wives home with them. During the Korean war, great numbers of our service personnel took their Rest and Recreation leaves in Japan, which became to them a kind of earthly paradise after the hell of war in Korea. During this conflict, our offshore procurement of military supplies in Japan gave that country's industry the boost it needed to break out of the doldrums of defeat and destruction and start on its way to what became the most outstanding instance of economic recovery in modern times. Japan began exporting to the United States and Europe a river of merchandise, much of which was of surprisingly high quality: cultured pearls, cloisonne, brocade, silk, cameras, binoculars, motorcycles, transistorized radios, portable T.V. sets, small cars, and mammoth ships.

A Japan boom of formidable dimensions was in the making. Hibachi, ikebana, o-shibori, kabuki, netsuke, ukiyo-e, kakemono, zen, tokonoma, fusuma, koto, shibui, haiku,maiko, sayonara, zori, shoji, happi (coats), sukiyaki, sashimi, and tempura became familiar words to many in this country. National magazines devoted entire issues to Japan. Japanese restaurants became popular and increased significantly in number. Japanese entertainers toured the U.S. with financial and critical success. More and more American tourists visited Japan, as did our military men en route to and from Viet Nam and other Far East stations. Hundreds of technical assistance tie-ups and joint-ventures between Japanese and American companies were formed. Ever increasing numbers of Japanese businessmen, students, exchange professors, and tourists came to the U.S. The vast majority of these were neatly-dressed men and women carrying cameras and transistor radios who were anxious to learn, eager to buy and sell, and ready to be friendly. They worked hard, behaved themselves, and left good impressions.

While we were becoming fonder of (or, in some cases, less bitter toward) the Japanese, they were becoming less *un*critical of us. But, on another plane, how does one ever really know what one people thinks of another? In the cases of America and Japan, the communications media of both countries have been largely discredited as exceedingly liberal and left-leaning. Contacts on the individual level probably produce no more than a handful of opinions tailored to favorable reception by the auditor. The techniques of the vast majority of opinion polls are still at the sophomoric level, e.g. questionaire interviewing.

Send an American opinion leader a questionaire asking if he thinks the Japanese are friendly, honest, hard-working, trustworthy, and he may answer yes, yes, yes, and, occasionally, no.

Try, however, the more sophisticated in-depth exploratory measurement techniques, and we will begin to see, as *Asahi TV* did recently, that many Americans associate the Japanese with lizards, cobras, alligators, and chameleons because they believe them to be cunning, sneaky, and deadly.

In any event, it would seem that Japanese opinions of us have, by and large, followed a down-hill path during the years since the immediate post-bellum era. Partly the blame is ours, but part of it should also be laid at the feet of their national capacity for resentment, which is based on a suspicion of their own inferiority in certain fields.

Because of a background of centuries of feudalism and their vertical social hierarchy, the Japanese have a tendency to feel inferior to those in higher social strata and, in compensation, to emphasize their presumed superiority toward persons in the lower strata. Having transferred this concept to foreign peoples and nations, the Japanese harbor an inferiority complex toward Westerners (which drives them to compete more strenuously) and at the same time feel superior to fellow Asians.

Shortly after the close of the war in the Pacific and the landing of our Occupation Forces, the Japanese realized that, contrary to their propaganda predictions, we were not going to rape their daughters or ravish their land. They saw we intended to leave their Imperial family and their mechanism of government essentially intact.

They had not expected this at all. They had been prepared for worse. When it did not come, their gratitude was heartfelt. The defeat had already caused many of them to jettison their traditional values and concepts en masse. The principles that they had been trained all their lives to respect suddenly became worthless. And into this vacuum marched the victorious Americans and their allies.

If they are nothing else, the Japanese are adaptable. Supremely adaptable. The same men and women who had planned with deadly seriousness to arm themselves with bamboo spears and charge our troops landing on their beaches now undertook, with equal dedication, to enshrine us as leaders, teachers, guardians, and elder-brother figures in the newly-emptied niches of their hierarchy. Since we had won the war, it was easy for them to conclude that ours must be, in many ways, a superior culture. They genuinely admired a victor, and the fact that we fed instead of slaughtered them suggested we were willing to enter into one of their traditional elder brother-younger brother relationships. (This is the "Winning Lord" Syndrome, which holds that the victor has specific responsibilities to a fallen foe who is properly subservient.) If so, then they were more than ready to become, as a nation, our younger brothers. The fact that, in later years, we did not always behave as they believed an elder brother should behave is a factor in the subsequent decline of our reputation in their eyes.

If only we could have withdrawn from the game after two or three years of Occupation and let the Japanese solidify their then existing opinions of us!

To the average Japanese, we were then a mythical race of magicians who could do almost no wrong. The very height of the pedestal on which they placed us made our fall from glory all the farther—and harder.

During the Occupation we made mistakes (such as the October 10, 1945 release from prison of 276 hard-core Communist leaders) that laid the groundwork for later events and conditions that were to contribute to the tarnishing of our reputation, although they were not apparent to many at the time of commission. The years after the Occupation witnessed a series of disconnected incidents (the Girard case, the Happy Dragon incident, the Sunakawa Base extension problem, the Kujukurihama Firing Range difficulty, the Mito Bombing Range dispute, etc.) that chipped away, bit by bit, at the fund of good will the Japanese held for us. Japan's non-objective press, with its mania for opposition to the political party in power in Japan—and to the United States, frequently gave such incidents a twisted emotional interpretation that illuminated the American role unfavorably. In this they were abetted substantially by Japan's irresponsible intellectuals, teachers, and students.

The visits of our nuclear submarines to the ports of Sasebo and Yokosuka inspired shrill and violent protests from Japan's hard core of professional anti-American agitators and gave the average Japanese, who was neither left-leaning nor anti-American, cause to wonder if our nuclear submarine visits were not perhaps a potential source of real danger to his country after all. Despite the fact that we had been responsible for the inclusion of the no-war clause in Japan's 1946 Constitution, we began to work for Japan's re-armament and participation in the free world's line of defense on the perimeter of Asia, which occasioned the Japanese to ask, How cynical can they be? Especially since most Japanese doubt that they would be in any active danger of a Communist takeover even if the U.S. withdrew its bases.

Our war in Viet Nam also raised grave doubts about our national purposes in the minds of many Japanese, even as it disturbed many Americans. For one thing, they tended to view it as a war of white men killing poorly armed Asians in their own homeland. For another, they feared they might be drawn into that war or into other U.S. conflicts in Asia against their will, because of American bases and sources of supply within their borders.

But more than any other single factor, the most contributory element in the deteriorating regard in which the Japanese hold us is simply over-exposure. Given our aims and commitments, some of it has been unavoidable—but not all. Too often our policies and actions have been guided by a persistent, fundamental American delusion: that to know us is to love us.

We tend to believe the down-to-earth, person-to-person diplomacy of the average American G.I., tourist, and businessman is such that foreigners, upon acquaintance, cannot help but be charmed; that although government-level relations may be strained, the common man in countries outside the Iron Curtain will at least appreciate and understand us if given a chance. We have an unlimited, almost child-like faith in the efficacy of our personal good will and generosity.

But in the case of Japan—and most other Asian countries, this assumption is false. Granted, all of them do not hate Americans, but to automatically and consistently assume that any Japanese or other Oriental will like us once he gets to know our man on the streets is a folk myth that is unfounded, unilateral, and downright dangerous. To substantiate this, one has only to gauge our popularity in towns near U.S. military bases in Japan in comparison to towns without American presence. Or to note the surprisingly large number of Japanese students and teachers who become anti-American after sojourns in our country.

I am reminded of what a Spanish general once said when asked to explain why he was restricting the free movements of his soldiery in Mexico some years after the conquest of that country: "If our soldiers were free to move about

Mexico, they would sooner convert the natives to their vices than attract them to their virtues." This has, I believe, considerable pertinence to many Americans who spend time in the Far East. Partly this can be blamed on extreme cultural differences: Our breezy, to-hell-with-tradition-and-formality approach does not set well with most Orientals. (Consider, for instance, the incident in which a prominent captain of U.S. industry asked the Emperor of Japan to autograph a ¥10,000 bill at a palace reception or the time when one of our vice-presidents gave voice to the Rebel Yell in the Taj Mahal.) Partly it can be blamed on language difficulties. And partly on the fact that many Americans are simply not well-behaved while abroad.

While quite a few of us were thus engaged in losing friends and alienating people, many Japanese commentators, reporters, writers, teachers, playwrights, movie-makers, and assorted intellectuals (who were wearing their locks long and scraggly years before our hippies discovered it as a badge of superior apperception) were having a field day working us over in print with no holds barred. Although largely uncoordinated, thousands of key Japanese in the communication media set out on a vengeful crusade to thoroughly discredit the United States. (Their individual reasons were many and varied, but prominent among them was the fact that the freedom to criticize had long been denied them. Once regained, they cast about for a likely target to test the sharpness of their knives on—and the U.S. happened to loom large in the field before them.) Because these scathing attacks were entirely in the vernacular, they generally escaped American attention. The number of Americans in Japan who could read the Japanese newspapers and magazines was—and remains—pitifully small, while the English language dailies either ignored these diatribes or toned them down. And few English-speaking Japanese wanted to upset their American friends with detailed accounts of what was going on.

Plays like *The Tachikawa Base: Ten Years of Rape* clearly suggested that the average American soldier in Japan was a confirmed rape-artist. Movies like *Buta to Gunkan* (Pigs and Battleships) delineated our sailors as a depraved, shallow, and foolish lot. Others like *Hiroshima, Nara Base, Konketsuji* (Half-Caste Children), *Kichi No Kotachi* (Military Base Children), and *Akasen Kichi* (Red-Line Base) were equally vitriolic and rancorous in their condemnation of Americans. Magazines like the respected *Bungei Shunjū* blamed us for a plethora of chicanery from the Japan Air Lines crash on Oshima to the Shiratori Incident in Sapporo. Other magazines, less respected but perhaps even more widely read, took us to task for anything their writers happened to be upset about that day. Many well-known and visible Americans—particularly entertainers—were a prime target, usually shortly after they had performed in Japan. That there was ever even a scintilla of truth in these reports is extremely doubtful, but when Paul Anka (a singer) visited Japan, for example, a Japanese magazine reported that he demanded a specified number of very young girls as part of his reimbursement for the trip and that he had his lustful will of them between numbers whenever he was performing. Frank Sinatra was said to have slept with eight hostesses at the Copa Cabana nightclub during one brief stay in Tokyo. Ava Gardner reportedly did a strip tease in a Tokyo "gay bar" and left her black step-ins with the bartender as a whimsical souvenir. Ad infinitum ad nauseum.

Denunciations like these clearly did not reach entirely unreceptive ears, since the Japanese have feelings of ambivalence about Americans, anyway. Most of them admire the materialistic advantages of our culture, our technological advances, and our comparative lack of guile, but they do not admire American racial prejudices, missionary zeal to convert the world to our way of life, and unemotional, "logical" approach to matters of mutual concern.

One issue of the *Asahi* newspaper, which I have before me, carries a most revealing article by Mr. Akiyuki Nozaka, a well-known author, commentator, and a remarkably candid and introspective man. I will not pretend that Mr. Nozaka's views are typical, for not many Japanese have analyzed and revealed their innermost selves with the stark frankness that Mr. Nozaka has. I do believe, however, that the contradictory aspect of his feelings may well be typical of most Japanese and that this very ambivalence is the confusing but nonetheless essential key to understanding their views of us.

This is what he wrote: ". . . When I see their (the American's) large bodies and healthy complexions and when I hear them talking, I become uneasy and emotionally upset. They cause me to act arrogantly without good reason or they cause me to smile at them flatteringly and obsequiously. At other times, they make me want to grind their proud noses in the dirt and rough them up. If one of them should come and sit down at my table in a beer-hall, I am sure that I would immediately become nervous and lose my composure. For that reason, I never wanted to go to the United States, but when I finally did go last year, I lost thirteen pounds in one week because I felt that I would lose my mind if I did not keep on drinking whiskey all the time.

"In comparison to the Americans, I am still convinced that the Japanese are an inferior race. Therefore, I become impotent when I go to bed with an American woman. Facing their men, I feel strongly that I am the underdog. I am ashamed of this, and when I come upon something at which the Japanese can beat the Americans, I grow ecstatic. . . . If a Japanese boxer wins over an American opponent, tears of happiness come to my eyes. . . .

"I sometimes wonder what I would do if we were to fight another war against the United States. If Japan were invaded and if an American soldier were to suddenly appear right in front of me, would I jump at him, using various judo tricks, even though I knew that I would be no match for him? Or would I smile slavishly and say, "Hello," "Thank you," and so forth? . . . .Sometimes I fear that I might act in the latter way. Now and then I lose myself in a reverie, masochistically imagining myself being thoroughly abused by Americans. I sincerely feel that I would rather dream my life away, like a lotus-eater, than for Japan to have any more dealings with America, even though it might mean that Japan would be relegated to the status of a primitive country. I pray that Japan will retire into a kind of hermit-like existence, because I do not want American democracy, freedom, or human rights. . . ."

Kenichi Takemura, a best-selling author and Japan's best-known TV commentator, says bluntly, "Japanese don't like foreigners, don't like foreign languages, and don't like foreigners intruding in Japan. Ninety-nine point nine percent of the Japanese can live without ever talking to a foreigner or ever buying goods from a foreigner."

There is, I think, much truth in what Mr. Takemura says.

Sure enough, they love to flood foreign markets with their exports, without importing all that much.

The Devil's
Language

After long, arduous efforts to master the language of the "heathen Japanee," Saint Francis Xavier reported to the headquarters of his Jesuit order in Europe that it must have been devised by Satan to prevent the teaching of the Gospel to the natives of that island empire. (Saint Francis first came to Japan in 1549. Four hundred years later, his withered arm made the trip again in a glass case, as a Holy Relic sent by Mother Church to be venerated.)

The Jesuits being missionaries of wide experience in learning foreign tongues and converting their speakers to the True Faith, one is led to wonder what it was about this particular language that so exasperated and thwarted the normally patient and kindly Saint Francis.

Japanese, which is kin to both the Ural-Altaic and the Polynesian lingual families, existed only as a spoken language until about A.D. 400, when Chinese books began to arrive in the Land of Wa, as the Chinese then called Japan. They also called it Ehr-Ban, which was written with two characters meaning the "source of the sun." In Japanese, the same two characters were pronounced Nihon or Nippon.

Showing evidence of their admirable adaptability even then, the Japanese decided that China's was a superior culture and that in order to profit from it and in order to retain the knowledge to which they were being exposed, they would have to possess means of recording it. Also, they were beginning to realize that their *kataribe* system

163

was not the most efficient method for retaining memory of historical events, familial lineages, etc. (The *kataribe* were a class of professional memorizers who were trained from childhood to learn by rote the names, dates, places, and events in Japan's history.)

Short of adopting Chinese in its entirety and abandoning their own tongue, the best way that the Japanese could see to provide themselves with a written language was to fit the Chinese hieroglyphics or ideographic characters to their native speech, and this they set about to do with enthusiasm. But to comprehend what happened and why Japanese became what has been called "one of the most effective barriers to mutual understanding that the mind of man has devised," the reader must bear in mind that this process of assimilation was at best haphazard, often indirect, long drawn-out, and riddled with inconsistencies. It was not, after all, as if there had been in the Chinese capital a Central Bureau for the Transmission of the Chinese Written Language to the Land of Wa or, in Japan, an Imperial Agency for the Reception, Codification, and Dissemination of Chinese Characters.

More than three hundred years passed from the adoption of the first character until the Japanese possessed a proper vehicle for recording words. Wars, natural disasters, and internal strife made traffic between the two countries intermittent and, at times, non-existent. Often the knowledge came slowly through Korea and was altered along the way. The Japanese scholars who were undertaking to learn Chinese writing and to select portions of it to fit to their native words were not restricted to one area but were scattered throughout Kyushu and southwestern Honshu, while some had gone to China itself to begin the process there. Chinese priests, scholars, and officials too came to the numerous centers in Japan from various parts of China, when China's spoken language was made up of more than two hundred recognizable dialects. As a result, a

Chinese from the old southern province of Go might tell the Japanese that a certain ideographic character was read or pronounced one way, while a Chinese from Kan in the north would read it with a different pronunciation and a man from To would enunciate it in a manner that bore little or no similarity to either of the first two.

If, of course, there had been a centralized, coordinated effort to absorb the Chinese characters, then a person at a suitable level of authority would simply have made the decision to use one or another of the several readings and to disregard the others. Unfortunately for us today, there was no such effort. While the Chinese from To may have been teaching Japanese Buddhist priests in the vicinity of present-day Kyoto his pronunciation of the character for, say, 'tide,' another Chinese from Kan may have been teaching Japanese scholars in Dazaifu in Kyushu his differing pronunciation for the same character. And so on.

To make the situation even blacker, Chinese pronunciations themselves changed during those three hundred years or so, as one Emperor sought to standardize the language and another neglected linguistic affairs entirely, so that a reading taught the Japanese in Dazaifu in A.D. 450 by a Chinese from To province might differ from the reading taught them in A.D. 650 by another Chinese from the same province.

This brings us up to the stage in Japan where we have one Chinese character that may have two or three Chinese pronunciations or readings and one native Japanese reading. For further confusion, now add two more ingredients: The Japanese version of the Chinese pronunciation was seldom perfect. What was said one way by the Chinese might, for example, have been said another by the Japanese, because the Japanese were incapable, without years of effort or childhood acquaintance, of accurately reproducing many Chinese sounds, and vice versa. Also, the Japanese sometimes decided to add a second or even a third reading of their own to the character. They might have been groping for a way to write a certain native verb, and, with no Chinese scholar handy to provide a new character for them, they may have decided to tack this verb onto a character they already knew, like an extra tail, because of a connection, perhaps only tenuous, between the two meanings.

As one consequence of all this, the Japanese of today must work with characters like 明, which has three Chinese readings (*mei, myō* and *min*) and five Japanese readings (*akarui*—bright, *akeru*—to open, *akasu*—to publish, *akiraka*—distinct, and *akari*—light), and like 生, which has two Chinese readings (*sei, shō*) and a whole raft of Japanese readings (*iki*—freshness, *hayasu*—to grow, as a beard, *fu*—a grassy place, *ki*—undiluted, *nama*—raw, impertinent, *nasu*—to bear, as a child, *shōzuru*—to produce, *ikiru*—to live, *umareru*—to be born, *haeru*—to sprout, *ikeru*—to arrange flowers, and *umi*—childbirth).

You may reasonably wonder how the Japanese reader knows which reading he should use. The general rule is to take the Japanese or native reading when the character stands alone and the Chinese reading when it stands together with one or more other characters to form a compound word. If there is more than one Japanese reading (as in the examples above), the reader can usually tell which to use by the *kana* (see below) modifications that are suffixed to it. A frequent difficulty comes in deciding how to read a compound word of two or three characters when one or two or all of them have more than one Chinese reading.

Take, for instance, the above character 明 for "bright," etc. with its three Chinese readings: *mei, myō,* and *min.* Then make a compound word by adding a second character 星 which has two Chinese readings, *sei* and *jō,* and which means "star." Such a compound would have six conceivable readings: *meisei, meijō, myōsei, myōjō, minsei,* and *minjō.*

The correct one happens to be *myōjō,* which means the planet Venus. (Literally, bright star.) This the foreign student must learn by rote, but for the Japanese child it is less difficult because he will already know the spoken word *myōjō* by the time he is old enough to have to learn its Chinese characters in school and so will not be tempted to read them as *meisei, meijō,* or what have you.

But this account of Oriental linguistic madness does not end here. The Japanese were finding that they had words for which there could be no Chinese characters: persons' and place names, for example, as well as objects and concepts that were uniquely Japanese. They considered tacking these, like still more extra tails, haphazardly onto the Chinese characters, as they had already done with entirely too many. But at last good sense prevailed. Enough was enough. There had to be another way.

It was then that someone suggested that they take about fifty Chinese characters, discard their meaning, and retain only the sounds. Then, when they came upon a native word (for example, *nichi*) that was in need of a way to be written, they could record its sound with two of the new characters-without-meaning: in this case, the one for *ni* and the one for *chi.*

Someone else protested, however, that each of these proposed phonetic characters contained, on the average, eight strokes, so that it would require forty or more strokes to write, for example, the five characters needed to represent the five syllables in the one word Shimonoseki (*Shi-mo-no-se-ki*). Whereupon another scholar proposed a sweeping simplification in the writing of each phonetic character to reduce the number of strokes from six or eight or ten to only one or two. For example, the character 利(for the sound *ri*) was reduced to り.

The Japanese now had fifty phonetic characters (later reduced to forty-eight) with which they could write all the sounds in their language. They called this syllabary *hiragana,* and not long thereafter they devised a second syllabary, which was even simpler but stiffer in stroke appearance and which they were eventually to use for foreign words, emphatics, and colloquialisms. This they called *katakana,* and they began to use both it and *hiragana* in the 8th and 9th centuries to write words for which they had no Chinese characters, to modify verbs, and to represent what might be called particles and prepositions.

A page taken at random from a present-day Japanese magazine, for example, will carry two or three times more *kana* (either *hiragana* or *katakana* or both) than Chinese characters. The characters represent the foundation, roof, and framework, while the *kana* form the siding, fixtures, flooring, window-glass, paint, and shrubbery of the building.

To illustrate an approximation of this in English, take the sentence, "The man walked to town." The ideas of man, walking, and town would be shown in Japanese with three characters, while the particle "the," the preposition "to", and the past tense ending "-ed" suffixed to the verb "walk" would be shown in *kana.*

Of the two *kana* syllabaries, the *hiragana* is the more cursive or flowing, while the *katakana* is more like printing. The Chinese characters too are written in gradations between stiff and cursive, the principal among these being *kaisho, gyōsho,* and *sōsho.* Going from the almost-printed style of *kaisho* to the so-called grass-writing or scribbled style of *sōsho* is somewhat akin to going into still another language.

With this the foundation of the Japanese language was formed, but Satan's work was not yet finished. There remained much addition, ramification, elaboration, and mystification to be added. The Japanese had only begun to build their society into the exquisitely formalized, pyramidal structure that it was to become, and the language had to be adopted to this structure—and, in turn, to assist in its control as a manifest gauge of degree of compliance and humility.

Spoken Japanese became not one language but several. Superiors used one set of pronouns, verbs, prefixes, suffixes, and verb-endings in speaking to inferiors, while inferiors replied in a different set. Words spoken between approximate equals differed from both of these, while words spoken to or about the Imperial family differed from them all. Male speech could be readily distinguished from female speech not only by a generally rougher tone and fewer polite forms but also by certain distinctive sentence endings, exclamations, and pronouns. Educated speech varied from the speech of the streets not so much in solecisms and malpronunciations (as is the case in the U.S. today) as in choice of vocabulary (staid and Chinese-y for one, racy and native for the other). Dialects developed, some for reasons to be expected in the natural growth of living language and others for political reasons. For example, the spread and use of the dread dialect of Satsuma or present-day Kagoshima were encouraged by clan chieftains to enable their border guards to detect Shogunate or Imperial spies from the north.

Although continuing efforts were made in the written language to codify the Chinese characters, no one, it seems, ever objected to the adoption of more. Attempts to reduce the number in use were almost unheard-of until modern times. As Western scholars today might flaunt their erudition by sesquipedalian tendencies and the use of French phrases or Latin derivatives in place of plain but effective Anglo-Saxon, the Japanese educated classes learned and used more and more Chinese characters as proof patent of their presumed superiority. This resulted in a written language that bore little more similarity to the spoken language than Latin does to modern Italian. With each new wave of Chinese learning (it ebbed and flowed) from the continent, more characters were adopted. And when Western knowledge poured into Japan after the Meiji Restoration, the Japanese had to dip again into their stock of Chinese characters to confect compound words (using the so-called Chinese readings) to describe Western ideas and objects that were new to them. A telegram was called a *dempō* or "electricity report"; a train became a *kisha* or "steam cart."

Many foreign words, however, were adopted as they were, and it was not until the xenophobic ultra-nationalism of the thirties and early forties that these were at last converted to Chinese compounds. To illustrate, the English word elevator, which had been *erebētā,* became *shōkōki* or "ascending-descending machine," and a pitcher of the baseball variety, which had been a *pitchā,* turned into a *tōshu* or "throwing hand."

The actual brush writing of the Chinese characters—and of the *kana*—became a highly respected art form. The more the writer was able to *kuzusu* (to break down, to write in a running hand) his characters, the harder his writing was to read and the more he was seemingly respected. Even today one frequently finds hanging scrolls on which famous calligraphists penned (or brushed) epigrammatic jewels that are illegible to the average Japanese and sometimes even to the owner of the scroll himself.

There remains one final ingredient that we must add to this mishmash before we can definitively depict Japanese as the thorny, difficult vehicle that it is: namely, the vagueness of the Japanese people themselves. Obviously, this is not the fault of the language. I can be just as exact in speaking Japanese as in speaking English, and I can be just as vague in English, if I choose, as most Japanese are in their own tongue. In fact, the few Americans who speak truly fluent Japanese may be more effective in that language than native speakers are, in the sense that they can avoid the burden of vagueness that the Japanese deliberately use to weight down their own vehicle of communication.

To the Japanese, vagueness is a virtue. To be exact is to be impertinent and arrogant, in that it assumes superior knowledge. To be vague is to be courteous and humble. Directness, especially abrupt directness, confuses the Japanese and causes them to *men kurau* or to eat their faces in consternation. To quote writer Sumie Mishima, "In the Japanese language exactness is purposely avoided."

This fondness for indirection is sublimated in the small poetic package called the haiku. English translation of two well-known examples are:

1.) "The world of dew　　2.) "Matsushima!
　　Is but a world of dew　　　Ah,　Matsushima,
　　And yet, and yet. . . ."　　Ah! Matsushima, ah!"

Just as the best novels are those that, by not telling all, invite the reader to participate imaginatively in the building of the tale, so the charm of haiku lies in what is left unsaid. In the words of famed Japan publicist Inazo Nitobe, "To give in so many articulate words one's innermost thoughts and feelings is taken among us as an unmistakable sign that they are neither profound nor very sincere."

This then is the final ingredient in the formation of the modern Japanese tongue: this preference for the vague, this fondness for indirection, this avoidance of the open declaration. Although more the fault of its speakers than of the language itself, the result remains the same.

Before the post-war language reform, the large Tokyo daily newspapers stocked between 7,500 and 8,000 Chinese characters in their type, and even the Rose-Innes dictionary with its 5,000 characters called itself a "beginners' dictionary." The first effort to reduce the number of characters in everyday use came in 1872, when it was proposed that they be limited to 3,167 specific characters. The list of these characters was destroyed in a fire, and the proposal came to naught. Four subsequent attempts were made in 1900, 1923, 1928, and 1939, when it was recommended by the Ministry of Education that the number of characters in common use be limited to 2,000, 1,962, 1,858, and 2,669 respectively. Nor did these efforts meet with any more success.

But in 1946, with the prompting of the Occupation Forces, language reform was again proposed by the Ministry of Education, whose list of 1,850 characters recommended for common use was approved by the National Diet the following year.

This more successful attempt not only limited the number of common characters but also simplified the writing of many of them. Further, it aimed at making the written language more closely resemble the spoken language, rationalizing the *kana* system (so that the sound *chō*, for instance, would be written with the *kana* for *chi*, *yo*, and *u*, instead of the kana for *te* and *fu*), gradually shifting the presentation of a written page from the old vertical format to the western horizontal, and popularizing the use of Romanized Japanese, with its resultant wedge into English familiarity.

At the date of this writing, the goals of this reform program have been achieved with varying degrees of success. The lesser success is to be seen in the efforts to popularize Romanized Japanese and to shift the format of the written page from vertical to horizontal writing, the greater in the rationalization of the *kana* syllabaries and the reduction of the number of the Chinese characters in common use, although indubitably many people must continue to read books written before the language reform of 1947.

Foreign words continue to enter the language (examples: *appakatto* for uppercut, *wan-suteppu* for one-step, *raito ranchi* for light lunch, and *kuraimakkusu* for climax), but twisted as they are by Japanese tongues, they are not much easier for the foreigner to understand than their purely Japanese equivalents would have been.

Standard Japanese is taken to be that of the educated class of Tokyoites, and while rural dialects are far from being extinct, increased social mobility, expanding education, and growth in the communication media have long since made Standard Japanese understood in the most remote corners of the archipelago without noticeable difficulty.

The Japanese typewriter, another of Satan's works, is a monstrous device of pedals, arms, levers, and sighting-holes which is used, if at all, more as a symbol of conspicuous consumption than as a popular, labor-saving instrument. It is being replaced by the word-processor.

Japanese today is a language spoken by the one hundred and twenty million citizens of Japan and understood, if not much spoken, by many persons over sixty or so in such Far Eastern areas as Korea, Taiwan, Saipan, and Guam, as well as in Brazil and our fiftieth state, Hawaii. In its spoken form, it bears absolutely no similarity to any of the dialects of Chinese (in answer to an oft-asked question).

Its sentence order (again different from the Chinese—and from English) is subject—object—verb, and the qualifying words generally precede the word they qualify. It builds up its words and grammatical forms with suffixes tied to the invariable stem or root. It avoids personification, and its elaborate system of honorifics often obviates the need for personal pronouns and for person in the verb. Its nouns have no number or gender, its verbs have no person, and its adjectives no degree of comparison. It is relatively easy to pronounce (its three mildly difficult sounds are the "*r*", the "*tsu*", and the double consonant, such as "*kk*" and "*nn*") and has little tonal pitch and less syllabic stress than, for example, English.

Granting that all the above combine to make, even after the language reforms noted, present-day Japanese one of the world's most difficult tongues for us to learn, the language is nonetheless done several injustices by foreigners with little or no acquaintance with it.

The first of these injustices is that visitors to Japan often assume, after brief experience, that it takes much longer to say anything in Japanese than it does in English. They may ask one short question in English and then be dismayed to hear their interpreter use five or six or even more Japanese sentences (or what sound to them like sentences) to transmit that one question to a non-English-speaking Japanese.

But what is usually happening in such instances is that the interpreter is using the additional verbiage to explain differences in customs and outlook. Let us say you visit Japan for the first time with a letter of introduction to a non-English-speaking Japanese businessman and that you call on him at his office with an interpreter. After several minutes of introductory conversation, you have the interpreter say to him, "I'd like to take you and your wife out to dinner tonight."

In Japanese that sentence should be no longer than it is in English, if as long: *"Komban anata to okusama o yūshoku ni oyobi shitai ndesu."* With only those words, however, the Japanese businessman may be puzzled. Why should this American visitor want to ask his *wife* out to dinner? That is unheard of. So the interpreter may have decided to offer the additional explanation that such an invitation is the custom in the U.S.—to forestall any puzzlement.

Even if you instructed your interpreter to translate only your exact words and nothing else (which, by the way, is not recommended), you might still have this apparently excessive verbiage. Suppose, at the restaurant you go to, you ask the Japanese businessman's wife if she likes, say, cottage cheese. The interpreter would say *kotēji chiizu* for cottage cheese, but he still might have to explain what it is, just as the Japanese might have to explain to you what bean-curd (English for *tōfu*) is.

Nor is it necessarily true that it takes longer to write anything in Japanese than in English. For instance, it takes us thirteen strokes to print "person," while it takes the Japanese only two to print their equivalent: 人. Four for "go" and six for 行, which means "go". Ten for "town" and seven for 町. Sixteen for "bridge" and sixteen for 橋. They average out to be about even.

Many foreigners throw up their hands in horror at the idea of learning the Chinese characters, which are admittedly formidable, but a recent study revealed that between 7 and 11 percent of American school children experience significant difficulty in learning to read, whereas the comparable figure for Japan is less than one percent. The cause for our poor showing is attributed to the abstract nature of our alphabet, in contrast to the pictorial nature of theirs. Our children simply have to learn, for example, that the letter A represents certain sounds, although they can see no apparent connection between the letter and the sound. We also have confusing "mirror-image" letters such as 'b' and 'd', while such words as "no" and "on", "was" and "saw" look somewhat alike but are in no way related.

In Japanese, the Chinese characters are direct descendants of pictures of the objects themselves. Notice how these pictograms evolved: from 屮 to ㄥ to 山 , meaning mountain. From ☉ to ⊘ to ⊖ to 日 , meaning sun. From 仔 to 子 to ƒ to 孑 , meaning child. From 丰 to 朼 to 木 , meaning tree.

Two or more of these pictograms could be fused to represent an abstract idea (or ideogram): Take a man

Without an intimate knowledge of their history, the pictograms by now strike us as overwhelmingly non-iconic.

in radical form and lean him against a tree 木 and we get the ideogram 休, meaning *yasumu* or to rest. Take a person 人 and put him in a box 囗 and we get 囚, meaning *shūjin* or prisoner. Take one woman 女, add two more 奻, and we have the ideogram 姦 for *kashimashii* or noisy.

Initially the Chinese characters may look like a wild jumble of strokes, dots, squares, and circles, but nevertheless there is method in this madness, and it comes from what is called the radical system. The characters are made up of one or more of 214 elements, which are also called radicals. The radicals often, but not always, serve to identify the character, at least in general terms. 木 is the radical for tree or wood, and any character containing this radical is likely to represent an object made of wood or a variety of tree. For example, 梯 means ladder. 板 means board, 櫻 means cherry tree, and 槍 means spear.

Knowing the characters in Japanese can be compared to knowing the root-languages of English (Greek, Latin, etc.), for then one has little trouble comprehending otherwise difficult vocabulary. I remember, for instance, that I was well along in my study of Chinese characters in school when we were given the compound word *nōmakuen* and its English equivalent: encephalitis. Although I had never met the word encephalitis in English, I understood the meaning immediately because I knew the meaning of the three individual characters for *nō-maku-en:* brain-membrane-inflammation. And during the many intervening years, I have often been able to understand the meaning of an unfamiliar word in English from its equivalent in Japanese, when the two were given side by side.

Lastly, I would call into question the ridicule that we sometimes aim at Japanese honorifics in cartoons ("Oh, honorable sir, so sorry, please.") and in books like *The Honorable Picnic*, in which altogether too many things were called "honorable this" and "honorable that". The Japanese honorific prefixes are "*o*", "*go*", and, rarely, "*on*". Only one or two letters, and just one syllable. Even if two or three of them are used in a sentence, they are hardly noticeable. But translate one of these short honorifics into the nine-letter word 'honorable' and cram three of them into one sentence ("Shall I ask your honorable wife to bring you some honorable tea and honorable rice?"—and the result is ridiculous.

Furthermore, the use of these honorifics often actually makes it possible to omit other words. If we are talking about hats (the word for hat is *bōshi*), you will know that by saying *obōshi* (honorable hat, as it were), I mean *your* hat and that by saying *bōshi* without the initial "*o*", I mean *my* hat. Without this device, I would have to say *anata no bōshi* to mean your hat, which is longer by six letters (or two characters) than *obōshi*, and *watakushi no bōshi* to mean my hat.

No matter how difficult it may be, the Japanese language is the one essential tool that the foreigner must possess to understand the Japanese people and their culture. About this there can be no question. Becoming fluent in spoken and written Japanese does not necessarily guarantee such understanding (although very few foreigners have learned the language well without having a great deal of knowledge about the customs and social attitudes of the people rub off on them), but it is the initial step—or mighty hurdle, if you prefer—that one must take if he is to travel the road that leads ultimately to significant comprehension. With the language as a tool, the student of Japanese affairs must go on to absorb as much as he can, both through formal schooling and first-hand experience or observation, of Japan's culture, politics, economy, geography, education, and society. Although his individual career plans will cause him to eventually emphasize one or two disciplines at the expense of others, he must nevertheless persist in a well-balanced multi-disciplinary approach to Japan, at least until a firm foundation has been constructed.

The number of Caucasian Americans who have become such "Japan Specialists" or who have become genuinely fluent in Japanese remains pitifully small, despite the several million Americans who have spent time in that country since 1945. (Of all the U.S. businessmen in Tokyo, only a handful are fluent enough to make an impromptu speech in Japanese.) As a result, we have today a situation in which there is an abyss of incomprehension between Japan and the U.S., an abyss that is much harder to cross from our side than from theirs. Here, as elsewhere, "language difficulty is at the root of more problems than man dreams."

Oddly enough, however, the first-time visitor to Japan may meet there an impressive number of Americans who are introduced to him as being "fluent in Japanese". Once an American businessman came to see me in Japan with a letter of introduction, and I met him at his hotel one day for lunch. While we were eating, he told me what he had been doing since his arrival and happened to mention that he had been invited to dinner the previous night at the home of an American, one Mr. Leonard, and his Japanese wife. I knew the couple quite well and listened with interest while the visitor told me about his evening there.

"I enjoyed myself very much," the visitor told me. "Say, Leonard speaks Japanese like a native, doesn't he?"

"Oh? I didn't know that," I said. (The Leonard I knew didn't speak much Japanese at all.)

"Sure he does. Wait now, are you sure we're talking about the same man: tall, about thirty-five, with a scar over his left eye?"

I nodded.

"Well, *that* Leonard knows Japanese, let me tell you.

Why, he talked Japanese to his wife all evening."

"Oh?"

"Sure, he has to. She doesn't speak a word of English."

With that, I changed the subject, but the point of the story is that Leonard's wife had graduated with honors from the English Literature Course at the Sacred Heart School, had won first prize in an English speech contest held among all college women in the Tokyo area, and had worked as a ticket saleswoman at the counter of an American airline. She knew a hundred, maybe even a thousand times more English than her husband knew Japanese.

What had happened, it later developed, was that Leonard was looking for a better job, and he and his wife were inviting every visiting American they met who might conceivably want to establish a branch office in Japan to their home for a carefully staged performance designed to demonstrate a highly-exaggerated version of Leonard's ability in Japanese.

If you meet ten Americans in Japan who are described to you as being "fluent in Japanese," you will be fortunate if even one of them approaches actually being so. The remaining nine will range from having almost no knowledge at all to a vocabulary of two or three hundred words in kitchen Japanese, often misused and mispronounced. The reason why such false reputations gain and retain currency is two-fold: One, it is the nature of the Japanese themselves to say that any foreigner who can ask for a drink of water in Japanese is very good in their language (*taihen ojōzu desu, ne*). In fact, in all my years in Japan, I can seldom remember hearing Japanese make of Americans such judgments as "his Japanese is poor," "he doesn't speak much Japanese," or "her Japanese is elementary." It seems that it is almost never in them to make such criticisms about individual foreigners. Two, the Americans in Japan who make or pass on such judgments seldom know enough Japanese to have any idea at all how much any other American knows about the language.

I myself know only five Caucasian Americans (I keep using the word "Caucasian" to distinguish them from Americans of Japanese ancestry who, for several reasons, are in a class by themselves) whom I consider to be well-qualified Japan Specialists or, if you prefer, Japan Area and Language Experts. (Genuine fluency in Japanese is implicit in both titles.) I have always had a deep interest in American students of things Japanese and have met many at the six Japanese language schools that I attended. Later, in Japan, I met or heard of others in my work and in my social contacts, so I believe that the five mentioned above must be a large percentage of the genuine experts to be found in either this country or Japan.

There are several cogent reasons why so few Americans have mastered the Japanese tongue:

1) The language is admittedly formidable. Not impossible, but definitely very difficult.

2) Since World War II, we have had no training programs, civilian or military, capable of producing such linguists. (The Defense Language Institute's full 47-week course is grossly inadequate; two and a half years should be considered the absolute minimum.)

3) During World War II several military language schools started at least two thousand Americans on the road to such linguistic ability, but very few of these students followed through on the start they had been given. For those who wanted to make a career of what we then called Japan Area and Language work, not enough rewarding jobs existed to justify their sustained interest, especially after the end of the Occupation. There were some jobs for historians, economists, sociologists, geographers, and what not—to which the desirability of Japanese language ability was added, like an afterthought, but almost none for

Japan Specialists as such. With few such jobs, there were few such Specialists. Or perhaps it was the other way around, like the question of the egg or the chicken. In either case, the result did not vary.

4) As a people, we take the learning of a foreign culture and language (except perhaps the familiar European ones) entirely too lightly. We simply have no concept of what is involved. Too often a foreign language for us is something to dabble in during high school or college or to study for four weeks in night school before an overseas assignment.

5) Anthony Burgess once said that the British are suspicious of linguistic ability, associating it with spies, impresarios, waiters, and Jewish refugees, and it is regrettable that we Americans are not entirely free of this taint, either. Only too often we tend to view with distaste and uneasiness any among us who become too intimate with a foreign culture and language, especially one outside the more acceptable French, Spanish, German, and Italian block. We suggest contemptuously that such Americans have "gone native." Art Buchwald, in his column from Paris, once quoted Air Force Major General W.T. Hefley as saying that he saw no advantage in employing American civilians who are familiar with a foreign country and its language. "If an American knows the local language," the general continued, "he may be injecting wrong ideas into his dealings with the natives."

The concerned observer of this comprehension gap between Japan (as well as other Asiatic countries) and the U.S. may well ask where the harm lies. Granting that we have almost no Americans who are genuinely expert in Japanese affairs, where and how does this hurt us?

For one thing, because almost none of our diplomats, businessmen, and foreign correspondents are qualified as Japan Specialists, we must rely on Japanese interpretation and translation for explanations of all that concerns both countries. Even assuming that the Japanese are honest in their attempts at explanation, we are still communicating on their terms and from their viewpoint. Although this is not always necessarily bad, it bears an analogy to a baseball team that must play all its games in its opponents' ball parks. Disadvantages, friction, and misunderstandings inevitably arise without our own team of experts to explain and judge, to analyze and advise—from *our* point of view.

Let no one think that no blunders, no crises, no tragic misunderstandings have marred the course of our relations with Japan since 1945. There have been only too many, beginning with some notable examples made under the auspices of the Occupation Forces and later encompassing government-level conflicts of interest, opinion, and policy that could have been solved or at least vastly alleviated by the placement of Japan Specialists in effectual positions. In the private business sector, the tragic mistakes are even more numerous. I know of more than twenty American companies that have failed in Japan simply because they did not seek the services and advice of Japan Specialists, evidently preferring to rely on men from their home offices who may have had, for example, a good record for selling soap in Hoboken but who knew next to nothing about selling soap—or even setting up a branch office—in Japan. Since such companies do not advertise their failures, I cannot help assuming that their actual number is much, much larger.

At the level of the individual American living in Japan, language frustration poses a very real danger. No American living in Japan who does not speak good Japanese can escape this danger entirely, except perhaps by spending all his time in those small islands of American culture there, such as the American Club and the Press Club. Elsewhere, he is continually beset by the thought that something is going on that he should know about but can't quite get to the bottom of. He strongly suspects that his secretary's explanation of the reason why the taxation office wants a new report on their office expenses for last year is not quite the whole story and that the maid's version of what the neighbor next door said about his wife is not entirely logical, but there seems to be nothing he can reasonably do to get a fuller explanation. And he is sure that those two Japanese toughs said something insulting to him and his Japanese secretary when they walked out of their office building together last evening, but she pretended not to understand whatever it was they said, so he hesitated to make an issue of it.

These are not isolated incidents occurring perhaps once a month. They happen every day. The more contact one has with the Japanese, the more frequently these disturbing questions arise. Even in his attempts to understand major events in Japan, the local American must rely largely on the four principal English-language dailies, which, it has been charged, avoid shocking their foreign readers with out-spoken and factual presentation of the news. Past Ambassador to Japan Edwin O. Reischauer often warned his American friends that they were wrong if they thought they knew Japan because they read the English dailies published there. (According to the *Atlantic,* Mr. Reischauer has also said, "I carefully read the best American papers and magazines, but, if I did not have an airmail edition of a Japanese language paper and other current materials sent to me from Tokyo, I would feel in the dark as to what is happening there. . . . I sometimes feel that, in our news-papers, Japan is the least adequately reported country in the whole world. . . . Its importance to us as our second largest trading partner in the world and our chief ally in Asia is obvious, but our press gives it far less space than to any of our other major allies. . . . We are served in our papers only the sketchiest outline of political developments in Japan, with little depth on important undercurrents, and a rather tired round of the same old color stories— Zengakuren, Sokagakkai, and neon lights on the Ginza—

but little of the real news of developing Japanese attitudes and actions that could well affect our future in Asia.")

Mr. Reischauer's point about the "rather tired round of the same old color stories" is well taken. Were we to add several more (Kabuki, geisha, Hiroshima revisited, flower arrangement, judo, cherry blossoms, the absence of street names, kamikaze cab drivers, karate, and Mt. Fuji), we would have boxed the compass, for these are the topics about which most of our non-academic writers on Japan concern themselves. Books that undertake to explain this alien culture to us are so few that one of the best (which is nonetheless imperfect) was written by a woman who had never been to Japan (*The Chrysanthemum and The Sword,* by Ruth Benedict), while another (*Things Japanese,* by Basil Hall Chamberlain) was written before the turn of the century and is still in frequent use, thanks, no doubt, to its lack of competition.

Again quoting the *Atlantic:* "James William Morley, director of Columbia University's East Asian Institute, lamented recently after a year spent in Japan, 'I can only say that it is shocking to return from that center of dynamism, which seems destined by every measure of educational, intellectual, aesthetic, economic, and political attainment and by every indicator of potential power to be not only *the* great power of Asia but, in the course of the next twenty years, to become one of the three greatest powers in the world, and find the American people abysmally uninformed and unprepared for the future this portends." The magazine's writer also supports Mr. Morley by saying ". . . as far as most Americans are concerned, their major Pacific ally (Japan) is all but unknown."

If we are to remedy this situation we must accept and regard Japanese Studies as a scholastic discipline within themselves, not as a fortuitous appendage to another discipline. Government and private industry should provide support for graduates of four-year Japan Studies programs, so that they can have at least two years of field work in Japan. After that, both government and industry could set up half-work, half-study apprentice programs, perhaps three years in length, in which the trainees could put what they learn to immediate practical use while being reimbursed on a reduced pay-scale. We should remove all contrived barriers to area and language familiarization (such as the State Department's ban on marriage to Japanese citizens by our diplomats) and offer positive encouragement, perhaps through a system of bonuses and allowances, to those trainees who immerse themselves as thoroughly as possible in the Japanese scene, living in average Japanese homes, eating only Japanese food, associating mostly with Japanese people, and so forth. More than anything else, we should establish high-level jobs for Japan Specialists in government, private business, the news media, and the military services. When such job opportunities exist, our young men and women will, I believe, begin to prepare themselves for those careers.

A Museum of Religions

The foreign visitor to Japan who asks a Japanese acquaintance to name his religious affiliation (a question not often asked among the Japanese) would be puzzled if the Japanese answers that he is both a Shintoist and a Buddhist.

Perplexed, the visitor might then refer to a book of statistics and learn that although the population of Japan is about 120,000,000, the total number of religious adherents is a surprising 195,000,000.

As this same visitor travels about Japan, he will be impressed by the outward evidences of religion, e.g., 185,000 buildings of worship, myriad roadside gods, torii, stone lanterns of deific significance, and odds and ends of other divine statuary, not to mention the millions of altars and god shelves in homes.

Yet if he pursues his inquiry, he may find the results of a survey conducted by the National Character Study Committee in which it was reported that 69 percent of the Japanese people do not consider themselves religious and that in the case of young people this percentage should be raised to 90. (In fairness, note should be made of a contrary theory that the Japanese are so profoundly religious that everything connected with simply being Japanese and living in Japan—from the smallest act of common courtesy and the obligations of *giri* to the leaves of the forests and the stones in the river beds—are sacred; that whereas the Christian may leave his religiosity at the door of the church, the Japanese carries his with him, deeply imbedded at subconscious levels. But if this is true, one wonders at the litter in the "sacred" aisles of trains and on the beaches and the spewing out of noisome pollutants into the "sacred" coastal waters and the atmosphere.)

Many years before this survey was made, however, Westerners had already characterized the Japanese as "irreligious," "indifferent to religion," "undevotional by temperament," and even outright "agnostic", although it should be borne in mind that these descriptions were offered from the standpoint of the Western world of Christianity, with its wrathful God who tramples out vengeance from the grapes of wrath and who keeps a sharp-eyed accounting of our many sins. When we see a Japanese bow before a temple or shrine with a smile on his face, we often rush to the judgment that here is an irreverent mocker ready to poke fun at the institutions of his shallow religion. When thunder, flame, and minatory predictions do not emanate from the pulpit or its equivalent, we may question whether this is really a religion or merely a set of easy-to-live-with accommodations casually but cunningly contrived by the Powers of Darkness. We suspect that a religion that does not stir, harass, prod, and exhort its adherents is one that will sit too lightly on their backs and will be too readily set aside when convenience or evil dictate.

This suspicion deepens when we learn that the Japanese have no equivalents of our day of worship or our Sunday church services, that their prayers pay more heed to form than to content, that they have no concept of a universal Messiah, that they (with the exception of the Nichiren Shoshu or Soka Gakkai people) do not seek to impose their creeds upon others through missionary activity, that they do not grapple with evil, that they are careless of the notion of a life after death, that their religious beliefs—(again with the exception of Soka Gakkai and its political arm, the Komeito) have almost no influence on secular or economic conduct, and that their religious holidays and observances are, by and large, continued and valued more as community gatherings and social events. In sum, we find that the Japanese have tended to mold their religions to fit their way of life more than the reverse.

But however heartily Christians may disapprove of—or at least view with darkling thoughts—Buddhism and Shintoism, the Japanese do not return us this courtesy, for their approach to all religions has been fundamentally tolerant and eclectic. Their persuasions—except Nichiren Shoshu and imported Christianity—are not mutually exclusive. Sometimes called a "museum of religions," Japan has generally, with only a few lapses, held its doors open to all religions that care to test their demotic appeal in the arena of their archipelago. Article 20 of their Constitution decrees that "Freedom of religion is guaranteed to all," and Japanese magistrates have upheld this provision with fairness and scrupulosity. Nor would it be just to assume that freedom of religion was a new concept force-fed to the Japanese by our forces of Occupation, since they were demonstrating a remarkable degree of religious tolerance four hundred years ago when they permitted Francis Xavier and the Catholic missionaries who followed him to proselytize freely within their boundaries and, again, nine hundred years before that when they embraced another alien religion, Buddhism, with pronounced fervor.

Not only do the Japanese permit all religions free entry into their land but most of them also allow at least two religions to enter their homes and private lives. The average Japanese will be taken to a Shinto shrine to be blessed shortly after he is born and in later years he will probably be married by a Shinto priest. When he enters school, his parents may accompany him to a Shinto shrine dedicated to the memory of a renowned scholar to pray for good grades. Should he become sickly, he may well visit either a Buddhist temple or a Shinto shrine that is known for its divine powers of healing. When he dies, a Buddhist priest will probably officiate at his funeral services and cremation, after which his ashes will find their final lodging in a Buddhist cemetery.

This religious parallelism is seen most clearly in the many homes that maintain both *butsudan* (Buddhist altars) and *kamidana* (Shinto god shelves), which may be serviced daily or only on days of particular religious meaning with offerings of food, flowers, and rice-wine and with incense and candles. Odd though it may seem to Westerners, acceptance of the rituals of two religions indicates neither confusion nor inner conflict in the average Japanese. He can live with both, and they coexist in peace and harmony and complement one another in strengthening and sanctifying the family, the community, and the nation itself.

The precedent for this pluralistic concept of religion dates back to A.D. 552, when Buddhism—in the form of sutras and images of Buddha sent as gifts by the King of Paikche in what is now Korea—first came to Japan, which had known only Shinto until then. Prince Shotoku (whose portrait now appears on one, five, and ten thousand yen notes) was able to convince his mother, the Empress Regnant Suiko, that Shinto and Buddhism would not clash with each other because Shinto was the religion of things past and Buddhism that of the future. This oversimplification does not quite hold water, but it was evidently sufficient to persuade the Empress, with whose blessing Buddhism was empowered to sweep through the aristocracy and subsequently to be exalted to the position of state religion. (It did not, however, actually become popular among the masses until the thirteenth century.) Buddhist priests further enhanced this syncretism by declaring ex cathedra that the gods of the Shinto pantheon were actually manifestations of the Buddhas (meaning persons who have achieved *nirvana* or enlightenment) already enshrined in Buddhist temples in Korea, China, and India.

An explicit example of this syncretism is to be seen in the

Kasuga Shrine in Nara, where the clan deities of the powerful Fujiwara family are depicted from both a Buddhist and a Shinto perspective.

It was India in which Buddhism originated but which is today held in spiritual thrall by other religions entirely. Gautama Siddhartha, an Indian ascetic, was born there in 466 B.C., the son of the ruler of a small agricultural republic called Sakya at the base of the Himalayas. At the age of twenty-nine he renounced earthly pleasures and set out to find universal truth, thereby becoming a Boddhisattva (one who is seeking truth). After attaining Buddhahood, he travelled about India for forty years teaching that man's sufferings are caused by his desires (one is reminded of Pascal's famous dictum, "The sole cause of man's unhappiness is that he does not know how to stay quietly in his room") and can be eliminated only by detachment. He told his disciples that the soul goes through a cycle of rebirths, the rewards of the next life being determined by the good works of the present one. Despite the implied possibility of pleasant existences, this cycle is basically one of distress. To achieve enlightenment is to end the cycle, and then all sufferings cease. His dying words were "All things are transitory." Nothing supernatural is attributed to his life.

The sutras—Buddhist scriptures that are usually chanted—were written in the succeeding centuries as the religion began to undergo many changes, the principal one of which was its division into Mahayana and Hinayana Buddhism. Mahayana or Great Vehicle Buddhism was the one that reached Japan at the date mentioned earlier, A.D. 552, and was adopted by the Soga clan as a tool in their rivalry against the Mononobe family.

Buddhism's subsequent thirteen hundred years of activity in Japan seem to reflect the very cycle of varying existences that Siddhartha taught. There were times when it was in absolute ascendancy and times when its future was indeed bleak. At times it was suffused with the gentle glow of art, harmony, good works, and peace, while at other times its bellicose monks from their temples atop Mt. Hiei descended like a pack of wolves in full cry on Kyoto and swept through the streets of the Imperial capital to emphasize their rigorous demands on the Court. But above all else the role of Buddhism during those long centuries should be remembered as that of the teacher under whose sometimes kindly, sometimes harsh tutelage Japan grew up. During much of that time all education and care of the sick were in Buddhist hands, and its practitioners introduced art and medicine and deeply influenced every sphere of social, political, and intellectual activity.

Although there has been a plethora of sub-sects and other splinterings in Buddhism, the present principal sects are Tendai, Shingon, Jodo, Shin, Zen, and Nichiren. The lay organization of Nichiren—the Soka Gakkai—is discussed under New Religions later in this chapter. Zen—the word itself means silent meditation—is apparently the most interesting to Westerners.

Zen Buddhism was established in Japan primarily through the efforts of two monks, Eisai (1141-1215) and Dogen (1200-1253), who brought it back with them from China. Its emphasis on self-discipline, austerity, and meditation appealed to both the samurai and the educated classes. Instead of scriptures or sermons, it depends on intuitive thought (as contrasted with intellectual speculation) which can lead to an aesthetic, instantaneously-achieved flood of apperception of the reality of the universe. This may be years in coming, but when, early or late, it is transmitted through a kind of spiritual telepathy, the believer is overwhelmed by this sudden revelation and can then enter into a condition of mystical self-intoxication which allows him to transcend consciousness of his Self and become one with the Universe. In this state, the mind of the believer becomes a holy void and he can ignore the vicissitudes and calamities of life, even as the Indian priest who brought Zen from India to China in A.D. 520 sat and stared in silence at a blank wall for nine years.

Zen is a philosophy of conduct like Camus' "sainthood without God." Its goal is to teach its believers how to live a transitory life with dignity and courage. The essence of its teaching is, "Look within thee; thou thyself art Buddha."

Before the advent of Buddhism in the sixth century, the only Japanese religion was a poorly-defined body of native rituals and beliefs that were without even a name. (Later it was called Shinto or the Way of the Gods to distinguish it from Buddhism.) The Japanese believed that there existed a spiritual essence in all animate and inanimate objects as well as in the forces of nature and even such phenomena as the echo. For one reason or another, they respected, even revered a great many of these spiritual essences, including some believed to exist in objects and forces neither pleasant nor beneficial. The more awe-inspiring, extraordinary, mysterious, superior, or even malignant the vessel, the more likely it was that the Japanese regarded its essence—its *kami*—with respect.

Some understanding of the word *kami* is necessary in any attempt to grasp Shinto. Originally it meant "above" and by extension, "superior." Because the Japanese bowed low before the objects whose spiritual essences they revered, these essences came to be called *kami*. Later, when Chinese writing was brought to Japan, one *kanji* or character (上) was assigned to the *kami* that meant above, while another (神) was given to the one that meant spiritual essence. Centuries afterwards, as Western learning began to flow into Japan, various English translations were made of the *kami* that originally meant spiritual essence, among them being mind, spirit, God or god, soul, deity, and superior being. When Christian missionaries sought a Japanese word to convey our concept of one omniscient Creator— for which there was no equivalent in any of the erstwhile

Japanese religions, they had no choice but to use *kami* (to which they added the respectful suffix *sama*). Our Christian God thereby became *Kami* or *Kami-sama*, but then this translation proved to be a two-way street. Upon learning that the Christian God was called *Kami*, other foreign students of things Japanese too readily assumed, when they heard a Japanese use the word *kami* in speaking about his own religions, that he meant God as we use the word. Not soul or spirit or spiritual essence or even god—but God. And if a Japanese happened to mention that he regarded his Emperor as a *kami* (the Emperor had this status while living), the Westerner interpreted this to mean that the Emperor stood in relation to the Japanese as God Almighty stands to us.

To be sure, the emperor of Japan was more, much more than what is implied by the two words "superior being." He and the emperors who preceded him stand very high in the Shinto Pantheon, lower only perhaps than the mythological group of deities that created Japan, but even so he could not be equated with the one supreme Christian Jehovah.

In addition to the long line of emperors, the spirits of winds, storms, rivers, mountains, and even stones were regarded as *kami*, as were deceased national heroes, famous scholars and officials, real and imagined ancestors, clan chieftains, and others. Toward most of these *kami*, the Japanese felt love and gratitude and often a desire to placate or console. They installed them in countless locations throughout the country and venerated them with offerings, prayers, and obeisances. They asked the intercession of appropriate *kami* for success in war, bountiful crops, and fertile wives. Prior to these acts of reverence, they were especially careful to cleanse themselves physically and to seek ceremonial purification after contact with such "defilements" as wounds, illness, sexual intercourse, menstruation, and death.

Each clan had a *kami* (called *ujigami*) which it came to

regard as its own tutelary deity. This *kami* may and may not have been an actual clan ancestor. If Clan A defeated Clan B in war, Clan A's tutelary deity assumed a position higher than that of Clan B in the rudimentary hierarchy of *kami* then forming. One particular *kami* of the sun (later called Amaterasu Omikami or the Sun Goddess) was the tutelary deity of a clan from whom the present Emperor is descended, and as the power of this clan rose, so rose the ranking of the Sun Goddess, who became at length the central deity in Shinto.

After the coming of Buddhism with all its gorgeous ritual, exalted moral code, impressive temple architecture, profound metaphysics, adventitious gift of a written language, body of sutras, history even then a thousand years old, and concomitant offering of arts and general knowledge, Shinto, as might be expected, went into a sharp decline. That the Buddhist priests did not stamp it out entirely is plain indication of the benevolent nature of their religion. Instead, they let it live and even recognized, as noted above, many of its *kami* as manifestations of their own Buddhas.

This stage of low posture for Shinto continued until about 1700 when a reaction set in and such scholars as Hirata, Mabuchi, and Motoori illumined the way for a national revival of interest in and respect for all that was old and all that was indigenous. Shinto was rejuvenated, while Confucianism and Buddhism were scorned. After the Meiji Restoration in 1868, Shinto's fortunes rose even more swiftly, for the new national government in Tokyo decided to utilize it as a tool in the accomplishment of one of their most important tasks: that of unifying the nation and instilling patriotism in the people.

During the Tokugawa Era, which ended in 1868, Japan had been a loose federation of small and large fiefs, the chiefs of some of which were closely allied to the Tokugawa shogunal family, the de facto rulers, by blood or marriage, while the chiefs of others were cool or even hostile to the Tokugawa and were held in check by a system of hostages, spies, heavy taxation, and, of course, military prowess. In theory, all Japanese paid homage to the Shogun in Edo and, beyond him, to the dim figure of the Emperor, surrounded by his often effete and sometimes poor court, in Kyoto, but in actual practice whatever loyalty the average Japanese could muster focused on the feudal hierarchy in his own fief.

With the restoration of the emperor Meiji, the fiefs were abolished and the *daimyō* or feudal lords dethroned. The dedicated leaders of the new government that had wrested control of the country from the Tokugawa dynasty realized that, in order to compete with the western powers which, led by the U.S., had shouldered open Japan's long-closed portals, they would have to inculcate upon the people a spirit of national unity and purpose and of patriotic devotion as well as an eagerness to strive and even to sacrifice self for country. Although they had an emperor at whom to direct this national devotion, his throne and glory were tarnished from long neglect. They were in need of an implement with which to restore, polish, and enhance his nimbus, and the implement they selected was their ethnic religion: the Way of the Gods.

One of their first acts was to divide Shinto into the subdivisions of State Shinto and Sectarian Shinto, with the latter retaining most of the religious aspects of the preceding form and the former becoming a supra-sectarian arm of government whose true purpose would have been more adequately revealed had it been named, say, the National Bureau for the Implantation and Promotion of Unquestioning Patriotism. In 1884, the government declared that State Shinto was not a religion at all but a cult, thus removing it from competition with proper religions, arranged direct and ample financing for its priests and facilities, and, as if it still had not made its point clear, forbade the priests from preaching any religious dogma.

It was as if the U.S. Congress had sponsored and financed a "Love America Society," in which all Americans automatically became members and whose leaders were charged with, among other things, the supervision of frequent recitations of the Pledge of Allegiance by all citizens and of properly respectful flag-raising ceremonies, management of Arlington National Cemetery, maintenance of historic battlefields, encouragement of military service and ardor, group singing of the Star Spangled Banner in theaters and other places of public assembly, and formal teaching of a glorified version of our national history in which many of our presidents and generals were raised to godhead status.

In December of 1945, however, our Occupation Forces caused the government of Japan to withdraw all official support from State Shinto, whose priests and properties thereupon coalesced with Sectarian Shinto. Correctly identifying State Shinto with the Establishment that lost the Pacific War, the Japanese people turned cool overnight toward their former national religion, and the priests and shrines that had subsisted on governmental financing found themselves in grievous monetary trouble. To eke out the scanty contributions from diminishing adherents, they converted part of their precincts into parking lots, kindergartens, and wedding halls. One—the Karasawasan Shrine in Tochigi Prefecture—began raising grapes, peaches, mushrooms, and hogs for the tourist trade and then expanded its income potential with a hotel and a golf course.

Nowadays, however, Shinto is regaining strength and has 102,000 priests in 85,000 shrines, together with some 91,000,000 adherents. Although it never had anything comparable to our Bible, its priests are now being trained to transmit to their parishioners a growing body of Shinto doctrine together with much of the traditional ethics that are no longer taught in schools. It has no images but uses instead symbols (for example, a stick with strips of paper attached to it) for its *kami*. It has no regular services, but ardent Shintoists may worship before the *kamidana* in their homes every day while the less devout may visit a shrine occasionally, especially on religious holidays and festivals. These acts of devotion at a shrine consist of rinsing the hands and mouth at the ablution basin, clapping the hands twice before the sanctuary to get the attention of the *kami*, bowing, praying silently, and leaving an offering. A priest may participate in more elaborate ceremonies, while the worshipper at home may only kneel, bow, and pray. The prayers are stereotyped expressions of appreciation and awareness of the bond between the living and the dead and between the individual and his community and nation. The worshipper does not specify his sins and ask forgiveness nor does he request certain blessings in return for which he will mend his ways. The central belief of Shinto is that man (e.g., Japanese man) is innately good and that he should follow his genuine natural impulses.

Shinto shrines can be identified by the *torii* set before them. These are gateways of two upright wooden or concrete columns topped by two more cross-pieces, the higher of which curves gently upward. There are usually three of them, and they progressively purify the worshipper as he passes through each. *Torii* is written with two characters meaning "where the birds are," but this does not refer to an occasional bird's preference for the cross-pieces as a roosting site but to an ancient custom of hanging from them dead birds as offerings to the *kami*.

In 1549, three Jesuit missionaries landed in Kagoshima

at the southern tip of Japan. To these Catholic priests, one of whom was St. Francis Xavier, must go the credit for bringing Christianity to Japan.

Between that year and 1635, these and other missionaries who followed did what was, on the surface at least, a truly remarkable job of converting Japanese to Christianity. In 1582, there were eighty missionaries and 150,000 converts in Japan, but by 1635, the year of the ultimate repression, the number of converts had grown to somewhere between 200,000 and 300,000 and included many *daimyo*, generals, and persons of cultural and material attainments.

Several factors, however, must be considered in connection with these reported conversions. First, certain similarities (candles, images, rosaries, altar flowers, incense, processions, and shaven heads of priests) between Catholicism and Buddhism led many Japanese to believe that the newly imported religion was still another of the numerous sects of Buddhism and, as such, had the approval of one thousand years of custom and familiarity. Second, the Japanese were quick to note that merchants with exotic commodities and firearms often accompanied the priests, so the many desiring to trade assumed that a warm welcome given the religious half of the team would result in reciprocity from the commercial half. Third, the priests devoted their staunchest efforts at proselytization to the feudal lords, who, if won over, sometimes ordered their subjects to become Christians en masse (and who were also known, when disappointed with the resultant benefits, to abruptly command their people to revert to Buddism with equal ease). Last, the Christian timing was apt, for the powerful Nobunaga Oda (1543-1582) was trying to unify the country and welcomed the Christians as a weapon for use against the unruly Buddhist monasteries in and around Kyoto.

Although Nobunaga's successor Hideyoshi Toyotomi was at first tolerant of the Christians and their activities, his benignity turned to dark distrust when he was told by Protestant traders from England and Holland that the Catholic missionaries were harbingers of Spanish soldiery, who would, as in the case of Mexico and the Philippines, come to conquer while the priests converted. In 1587, Hideyoshi issued an edict banning Christianity but did not begin to enforce it until ten years later, when he had nine Catholic missionaries and seventeen Japanese converts crucified. (The Japanese courage and equanimity in the face of this difficult death is said to have exceeded that of their foreign mentors—the first time that Catholicism had encountered such fortitude in non-Europeans.)

Hideyoshi died before he could carry out his intent to suppress Christianity, and his successor Ieyasu Tokugawa was at first too beguiled by the potentialities of trade with Europe to take up the cudgels himself. At length, however, he too became suspicious and then antagonistic and so initiated a series of repressive measures that culminated in the massacre of more than 30,000 Christian converts in Shimabara in early 1638. (Some authorities believe that the Shimabara Rebellion drew as much momentum from economic and political unrest as from religious differences, that it just happened to take place in a district in which many Christians lived.) Be that as it may, the rebellion brought on the expulsion of the missionaries, an absolute interdiction against all Christian converts and activity, and the closure of Japan's gates (except for a handful of non-Catholic European traders on the island of Dejima) to the world for more than two hundred years.

Although the motives of many of the Japanese who embraced Christianity during the years between 1549 and 1683 may be questioned, there can be little doubt that at least some of them had faith of the highest and firmest order, for within a month after the construction of a Roman Catholic church in Nagasaki in 1865, four thousand Japanese Christians from the nearby village of Urakami came to the church to rejoice and to explain to the priest that they and their forebears had secretly kept the Christian faith alive for 225 years. Although Japan was then in the process of opening its doors to the West, the laws against Christianity were still in force, and the Tokugawa Shogunate arrested all four thousand and banished them to other feudatories. Fortunately, the Tokugawa regime collapsed before more serious harm could befall this stout-hearted assemblage. Ironically, the same Catholic church, which the four thousand faithful from Urakami later joined, met complete destruction at our hands when we dropped the second atomic bomb on Nagasaki in August of 1945.

With the fall of the Tokugawa government and the restoration of the Emperor Meiji, there began a cycle of fair and foul weather for Christianity in Japan. In 1872 the Meiji government lifted its ban on Christianity and allowed free missionary activity, but it was not until the 1880's that Japan began to fully realize how much it would have to learn from the West. In the massive importation that soon followed, not only was Christianity included but it became, in fact, so popular that one prominent magistrate was prompted to predict that it might even be named the official state religion.

During the 1890's, however, reaction set in and a rising tide of nationalism dampened Christian prospects considerably. Then the sight of Christian nations slaughtering each other in the bloody baptism of the First World War aroused serious doubts in the minds of the Japanese about the efficacy of Christianity and the sincerity of those who embraced it, but the humanitarianism of Wilson's Fourteen Points and the fast, unstinting aid we sent to Japan after the Great Kanto Earthquake of 1923 helped restore some of its prestige. Unfortunately, the passage of the Oriental Exclusion Act by the U.S. Congress in 1924 nullified these benefits and Christianity again went into a decline, which was hastened and lengthened by the crescive xenophobia of the 1930's.

As might be expected, the Allied victory in 1945 re-awakened an interest in Christianity and led to an abolition of all restraints on religion. Even so, the number of native Christians in Japan today is only about 930,000, well under one percent of the population. Approximately forty per-cent of these Christians are of the Roman Catholic per-suasion and four percent Eastern Orthodox. The re-mainder are Protestant, if we include in their ranks the 75,000 members of the "Churchless Christian Movement" begun by Kanzo Uchimura.

That Christianity has not fared better in Japan must be attributed to the exclusive nature of the religion, which isolates its converts from the community around them, and the traditional preference of the Japanese for a less for-bidding religion that allows for their weaknesses.

Indeed, a Japanese could borrow the words of William Blake to explain his avoidance of a Christian church:

"If at the church they would give us some ale,
And a pleasant fire our souls to regale,
We'd sing and we'd pray all the livelong day,
Nor ever once wish from the church to stray."

It is estimated that one in every five Japanese is an adherent to one of the 171 so-called "New Religions," one-third of which can be loosely classified as Shintoist, one-third as Buddhist, and the remainder as a jumble of miscellany. Once included among this miscellaneous classification but now sadly defunct were *Denshinkyō*, whose believers worshipped electricity and Thomas Alva Edison, and *Bosei-kyō*, whose followers regarded sexual acts as primary healing agents.

Although they may have had much older roots, most of these New Religions rose to prominence after the end of World War II because their believers were disenchanted with the theretofore established religion (Shinto), and because Occupation-inspired reforms freed all genuine religions from the trammel net of the 1939 Religious Bodies Law.

Obviously, when one is speaking of that number of separate religious entities, there must be considerable variance in size, organization, belief, ritual, and congregational make-up, but nonetheless some generalizations can be made that have application to most of them. They have, for example, tended to concentrate their initial efforts at proselytization on farmers and workers, later advancing on the middle classes. The organization, direction, and control of their priests are less formal than in the older religions. They draw their theology from several, sometimes many sources. Their doctrine and philosphy are weak. Their appeal is based on hope for a better life and on ritualistic or magical curative powers. They have strong leaders. (In sixty or so of the 171 New Religions, the leaders have laid claim to divine inspiration or revelation.) With the notable exception of the Soka Gakkai, they are tolerant of other religious creeds. They are easy to understand and easy to join. They have their own Meccas in Japan. They preach that their promised rewards can be enjoyed in this life. They offer highly emotional ritual performances. They appeal to unsophisticated persons who may have suffered grievous bereavement or injury or who have lost their convictions about the purposes of life. And they implant in their followers a feeling of personal dignity and importance.

Although the New Religions have often been contemptuously ignored or belittled as appealing only to the ignorant and superstitious, some authorities regard their rapid growth and incontrovertible vitality as one of the three most significant developments in the history of Japanese religions (the other two being the adoption of Buddhism beginning in the sixth century and the rise of the demotic Buddhist sects in the thirteenth).

Chief among the New Religions, in descending order based on the number of their devotees, are the Soka Gakkai, Reiyukai, Tenrikyo, Rissho Koseikai, and Seicho no Ie. The first—the Soka Gakkai—is the one that has attracted the most foreign attention.

Contrary to the implication in its name, the Soka Gakkai (Value-Creating Learned Society) appeals more to persons of lesser learning than to the intelligentsia. It is a phenomenon that has amazed Westerner and Japanese alike. In Japan, it boasts a membership of sixteen million souls, while in the U.S. (where it goes by the name of Nichiren Shoshu or the Orthodox Sect of Nichiren) its believers number 170,000, with most of the more recent converts being Caucasian. Its political arm in Japan is the Komeito (lit. "openly illuminated party" but usually given in English as the Clean Government Party), which is now Japan's third strongest political organization. It is the fastest growing major religion in the world.

Nichiren (1222-1282) was one of the most colorful and turbulent figures in Japanese history. A monk of the Tendai denomination, he became dissatisfied with his and other Buddhist sects and founded the first distinctively Japanese branch of that religion. Preaching that the Lotus Sutra was the perfect revelation of truth and the only written words his followers need know, he stormed through Japan vilifying all other religious beliefs. He sought to appeal to the common man by identifying religion with natural life. His powers of mystical prognostication won fame when the Mongol invasion that he had predicted became a reality. His impassioned preaching and dire warnings stirred much religious fervor and unrest, for which he was exiled and even sentenced to death. (He was spared, almost miraculously.) When he was past fifty, he had a loose tooth removed and handed it to Nikko, his leading disciple, instructing him to use it in spreading the true gospel as Nichiren conceived it. To this molar was attached a bit of flesh, which has reportedly grown until it now covers nearly all of the tooth. Nichiren is said to have predicted that when the tooth is entirely covered, the religion he fostered will have reached its zenith.

After his death, Nichiren's faith splintered into thirty-one groups. One of these—Nichiren Shoshu—is the spiritual parent of the Soka Gakkai, which was established in the early 1930's by a schoolteacher named Tsunesaburo Makiguchi, who had little success in popularizing his beliefs and died behind bars. His successor Josei Toda, however, found the religious freedom of the post-war era more receptive to propagation and growth and by 1951 he had assembled under his guidance five thousand devotees. When Toda died in 1958, the mourners in his funeral procession numbered more than three hundred thousand. Daisaku Ikeda, a man of lusty appetites, succeeded him.

Much of the Soka Gakkai's appeal derives from excellent staging and its emphasis on quick rewards. ("If you sincerely wish for something hard enough while chanting over and over *'Namu Myōhō Renge-Kyō'*, you will surely receive it.") Its success at myriad conversions can be mostly attributed to *shakubuku*, the word the society uses to encompass its efforts to convert non-believers. Literally, *shakubuku* means "to shatter and subdue," referring to evil spirits and not the intended convert, although visual evidence may sometimes suggest the contrary.

Since each Soka Gakkai member has a quota of converts that he must bring in or face serious disapproval, *shakubuku* can be a formidable—even frightening—affair. The Japanese wife of an American friend of mine in Tokyo is a member of the Soka Gakkai, and she has furnished me several close looks at the methodology. When individual attempts on the part of a member have failed to bring a target to his senses, he summons aid. If the ardent efforts then of a group of six or eight bright-eyed fellow-members are still unsuccessful, they may resort to such means as standing in front of the target's residence in the evening and chanting prayers for his soul for hours on end. And should the convert-to-be still be uncowed, his neighbors may even join in the chorus of exhortation, if only to achieve peace in the neighborhood.

Of late, however, the sect has applied the soft-pedal to some such methods, now that the Soka Gakkai is growing out of its fitful adolescence and nearing a form of maturity.

In part, the Society's success in politics (it leans to the right but exploits the weaknesses of both the right and left) can be explained by their use of tactics similar to the ones used in *shakubuku* and partly by the fact that their political arm, the Komeito, became active when the "black mist" of corruption was raising its heinous head somewhat higher than usual in Japanese politics. Also, by the statement of a Komeito political worker who said, "In winning the election campaign, we simply disregarded the election laws. Since our efforts serve the Soka Gakkai, what we did cannot be wrong." The police did not, however, always take this view and so arrested many members. The Komeito candidates nevertheless won and were seated in the Diet.

When it comes to denouncing other religions, the Soka Gakkai believers are not at all hesitant or retiring. Nichiren himself declared about three other Buddhist sects, "Zen is a religion of devils, Shingon means national ruin, and the Risshu congregation is a pack of traitors." About Christianity, modern-day Soka Gakkai says, "Jesus died on the Cross. This fact is proof that he was defeated by his opposition. . . . But when he was about to be beheaded, our Saint Nichiren shouted to his executioner, 'Time is passing. Be quick about it! Cut off my head!' No sooner had he said this than the gods of the universe came to his aid. Meteors shot across the sky. Thus did Saint Nichiren beat his enemies. Comparing this vitality with that of Jesus, we see that Christianity has no power." About Shinto it comments, "Shinto is a heretical religion that we must destroy." And it calls Tenri-kyo an "absurd and good-for-nothing religion."

In its struggle to grow, the Soka Gakkai once locked horns with Tanro, the giant coal-miners' union, which had viewed the role of religion in the life of its miners with cool indifference. In 1953, the Society had only a hundred or so members among the miners on the northern island of Hokkaido but by 1958 this number had increased to more than one hundred thousand. Seeing the dangerous, insecure life of the miners as fertile ground for sowing their seeds, the Soka Gakkai had promised the miners an end to mine accidents, effortless wage increases, good health, and spiritual happiness. When the situation reached the stage of crisis, the Tanro union began to intensify its resistance to this attempt to usurp its traditional role and authority. Their main counter-measures consisted of pointing out the more glaring fallacies in the Soka Gakkai teachings, publicizing the names of miner-converts who were still mysteriously ailing or poor, and suggesting that the more vociferous of the new adherents among the miners volunteer for especially hazardous mining tasks, inasmuch as they were presumably protected from all accidents by the Soka Gakkai's escutcheon and promises.

The fact that not many miners volunteered proved to be rather effective in checking the Soka Gakkai's subsequent growth in that segment of Hokkaido's population.

Child-bearing Housekeepers?

A great many American men have married Japanese women since the close of World War II, and this number would assuredly be larger if, during the Occupation period, our military authorities, mindful of possible opposition to such marriages back home, had not placed formidable obstacles in the path of such proposed unions.

Further, the number of Japanese women who have been full-fledged mistresses of Americans living in Japan is even more numerous while those who have associated with Americans, to varying degrees of intimacy, must, of course, exceed that.

After all, millions of Americans have lived or sojourned in Japan since 1945, and the single (as well as more than a few of the married) men among them probably became acquainted with—let's be conservative—two or three Japanese women while in their country.

Admirers of the Japanese female say that this is ample proof of the worth of the species. Cynics, on the other hand, quote the American sailor who, after many months on Nagasaki station before the war, said, "The longer I was out here, the whiter they got." But whichever view prevails, there can be little doubt that Japanese women are different—and that they are changing.

Physically, they tend to be petite, graceful, energetic, and fine-skinned. On the minus side, their legs are too often short, heavy, and slightly bowed, but the practice of strapping babies to their mothers' backs for ease in carrying is diminishing, so the last characteristic should become less common in the future. Their noses are low, while the Mongolian folds at the inner corners make their eyes appear slitted and far apart to us. Both of these facets, however, are being revamped in large numbers daily in the more than three hundred (seventy in Tokyo alone) cosmetic surgery clinics and hospitals throughout the country, while improving nutrition together with new concepts of baby-care and -feeding are giving them taller bodies, long, slimmer legs, and better vision. (It is common these days for 14 or 15-year old children to be taller than their parents.)

Go to the Ginza on a warm Sunday afternoon—the stores are open then—and observe Japanese femininity at large. Stroll along for an hour or so and you will see some of Japan's loveliest women. Slim, gay, clean, tastefully dressed mostly in Western clothes, and not too heavily made up, they are light-years apart from the "beauties" of Japan's past.

A typical beauty of the Heian Period (794–1185), for example, would have worn her hair five yards in length and blackened her teeth; she would have shaved her eyebrows off and coated heavily with white powder that part of her body which aroused her male admirers as erotically and effectively as deep cleavage today excites the breast-minded American male, e.g., the nape of her neck, and she would have walked pigeon-toed with a mincing gait, which is still common in women wearing kimono and *zōri*.

Even today the Japanese man's concept of female attractiveness differs largely from that of his Western counterpart, which is a fortunate circumstance for some of us, for we can often find the most comely girls languishing away for lack of suitors in out-of-the-way Japanese towns: girls who, because of their height or their higher noses or their more-oval-than-round faces, are amenable to sharing their neglected attributes with foreigners, in lieu of local lovers.

Once in Yokosuka, I knew an American navy officer who went boar-hunting in Miyazaki Prefecture down in Kyushu. Instead of boar, he came back with one of the three most stunningly beautiful Japanese girls I have ever seen. She was only eighteen and spoke little English, but theirs had been a case of intense mutual attraction from the start.

With hardly a word to her parents, she had packed a suitcase and followed the navy officer, who was a tall, clean-cut young man from an old New England family, back to Yokosuka. Obviously, they were deeply in love with each other and oblivious to much that went on around them, but inability to communicate adequately—at least, not in words—forced them to call on me frequently for interpretation. During these meetings, her utter lack of feminine wiles and her charming, pristine innocence became obvious and incontrovertible. When I learned that she had never before even had a date with a boy, I expressed my surprise, so she explained that it was because people thought she looked *okashii* (funny) and *gaikokujin-kusai* (foreign).

I lost track of the couple soon thereafter, but I heard he married her and took her home with him.

Much of the controversy about Japanese women spins around the pivotal question: how subservient are they to men? Are they merely child-bearing house-cleaners who are, in the words of Tennyson: "something better than his dog, a little dearer than his horse?" Or, are they, as some would have it, calculating creatures with velvet-covered claws and hearts of steel? And, whichever they are, what made them that way?

The tradition of male dominance did not always obtain in Japan, there having been clear-cut matriarchal overtones at times in their distant past. The highest deity in their Shintoist pantheon of gods was Amaterasu-Omikami, the Sun Goddess, and, going from mythology to ancient

Chinese records, one finds such commentaries as, "The Japanese formerly had kings, but after years of civil war, they agreed to set up a woman named Himeko as their sovereign. When Queen Himeko died, a great mound was raised over her and more than a thousand of her attendants followed her in death. Then a king was raised to the throne, but the people would not obey him, and civil war broke out again. A girl of thirteen, a relative of Himeko, named Iyo was then made Queen and order was restored."

About A.D. 200, the Empress Jingo, whose martial ways may have inspired our English word "jingoism," led Japan to its first successful foreign conquest (of part of Korea), a feat that no Japanese man was to match for seventeen hundred years.

Nor were these instances of female leadership exceptional. The names of such Empresses as Koken, Komyo, and Suiko figure largely on the pages of early history. Then, in the late twelfth century, there arose the Lady Masako Hojo, who was surely one of the most competent and strong-minded women of any age or any country. On the night of her wedding to a Taira governor, she eloped with the renowned warrior Yoritomo Minamoto and ruled Japan at his side until his death in 1199. Thereafter, as the *Ama Shōgun* (Nun General), she ruled Japan wisely and well, from several stances, until her own death in 1225.

At the beginning of the Muromachi Era (1392–1573), Japan entered a period of gradually-worsening lawlessness and confusion, a time that contrasted sharply with the previous centuries of comparative order and peace. Divisive currents flowed strongly, old loyalties and ideas were uprooted, relatives battled each other in sporadic but savage outbreaks of violence. When the heads of families and clans died and divided their holdings equally among their sons and daughters or perhaps left the reins of the blood kinship group in the hands of an only female child, this often resulted in the diminution of the property and the dissolution of the unit. The women were just not strong enough to fend off the physical inroads against them and to hold the unit together. Of necessity, the family heads and clan chieftains came to choose sons to take over and preserve unity. If they had no sons, they adopted them from other families, preferably blood-related but often not, a custom that persists today.

This, then, was the beginning of the downward road for Japanese women, and the slope was made more precipitous by Buddhist precepts that women were fundamentally more prone to sin than men and that their only path to expiation lay in total subservience to the male element.

How far downhill did she ultimately go? To that lower level where, in the traditional ideology, she not only obeyed her husband and master in everything but also "enjoyed" every minute of it. She had no rights, only duties. Her pleasure came not from establishing her own independence and dignity as a human being but from learning to do what she had to do as a woman. In life, she had three masters: her father while young, her husband during the middle years, and her son or sons in old age.

If her husband proved unfaithful to her, she could take no legal action against him, but if she was caught committing adultery, both she and her lover could be crucified.

In time, her position became like that of the American Indian squaw in that oft-told anecdote: On a hot summer day, a white man saw an Indian brave riding a horse with his squaw walking along behind in the dust. The white man asked why she wasn't riding. The male Indian's reply was eloquently brief and to the point: "She no got horse."

This is also remindful of the story I heard in Korea during the war there: An infantry private fresh from the States said he had been told that the Korean men were very considerate of their womenfolk, that they often permitted the women to walk ahead of them. A sergeant with more experience answered, "Yeah, but only through the minefields."

Proverbs, which are often accurate weathervanes of popular attitudes anywhere, reflect the discredit done Japanese women: *Onna wa mamono* (Women are demons.) *Onna-gokoro to harubiyori* (A woman's mind and spring weather, e.g., both are too changeable.) *Onna no saru-jie* (Woman's monkey-like wit.) *Onna-hideri wa nai* (There is never a dearth of women.) *Onna sannin yoreba kashimashii* (Three women together make a terrible clatter.) *Onna wa sangai in ie nashi* (A woman has no home in any of the three worlds.) And the most cynical of all: *Shichinin no ko wo nasu tomo onna ni kokoro no yurusu na!* (Never trust a woman, even though she has borne you seven children!)

Her chief aim in life, it was held, was to bring comfort and happiness to her husband, to his parents and other relatives, and to her children. She married at the command of her parents and was ruled by her husband's every wish and whim. She was the first to arise in the morning and the last to go to bed. In the evening, her husband bathed first, the children next, and she last. If some of the more tasty dinner dishes were in short supply, they were distributed in that same order.

In olden times, her husband could divorce her simply by giving her a *mikudari-han* (lit., three-and-a-half lines): a letter of notification of intent, only three and a half lines in length. In more recent times, all that was required was a trip to the ward or town office where the family register was kept and the obliteration of her name. Seven reasons were considered acceptable. Among them were talkativeness, a communicable disease (house maid's knee or the itch perhaps?), jealousy, and refusal to serve her husband's parents.

She didn't dream of going out with her husband for pleasure; if they had to attend a de rigueur social function (such as the wedding of a relative) together, she was expected to walk three paces behind him, stay clear of him during the reception following the wedding, and speak only when spoken to in mixed company. (Ah, those Good Old Days!)

If, despite her best efforts, he nevertheless divorced her, her chance of making another marriage was slim indeed. *Demodori* (girls who have "gone out and come back") were rated only one notch above cripples and *Eta* (pariahs)in order of desirability.

Shortly after the end of the Pacific War, I was invited one evening to have dinner at the home of a professor at Kyushu Imperial University. A woman in a rather shabby kimono answered the door, asked me to come in, took off my shoes for me, and guided me to the room where the professor awaited my arrival. Then she bowed and withdrew, only to appear again from time to time with drinks, ash trays, peanuts, rice-crackers, and other offerings. The professor did not introduce her to me and because his tone when speaking to her was abrupt—almost angry, in fact— I was half-convinced that she was a maid. (This was one of my first visits to a Japanese home, and I was trying to learn by watching in silence rather than asking questions that might prove embarrassing or inappropriate.) When at length dinner was served, this same woman served us but did not sit with us at the low table on the tatami mats, which persuaded me that she was, after all, a maid.

Thereafter, I'm afraid, I began to talk to her as I would talk to a maid myself. In polite enough language, of course, but not in the words that one should have used to the mistress of the home. And, as you have already guessed, it turned out that she was the professor's honorable wife.

We may wonder why the Japanese woman endured all this, why she did not demonstrate, confront, and even revolt? The answer reflects economic necessity. She could be divorced at almost any time for even whimsical reasons.

The word alimony represented an unheard-of concept. Any money she got from her husband was prompted by his generosity—again, whimsical—and not by force of law. (And it was almost always comically inadequate.)

As a woman who "had gone out and come back," she had but little chance of another marriage, especially not of a decent one. She seldom had the skills needed for gainful employment, but even if she did, she would most probably have been forced to quit work at the age of thirty or so, to make room for a male employee. This practice is still common today. Work for a woman is widely regarded as something to fill the brief time-gap between school and marriage, not as a means to support herself for more extended periods. If she was one of the lucky few who came from affluent homes, she went back to her parents to wait out her years in physical, if not spiritual, comfort. Otherwise, she became a servant or a member of the *mizu shōbai*: that nether world of drinking establishments, geisha houses, and restaurants where a man can enjoy food and drink and usually women.

So she "endured the unendurable" and stuck it out with her husband. Of course, such a life was not entirely without its compensations. The husband usually was not an insensate brute. Although he held the whip, he did not always use it, and even though he would have thought it unmanly and degrading to tell her that he loved her, he may have demonstrated sincere affection for her in other ways. The pages of Japanese history and literature are liberally sprinkled with accounts of extreme examples of mutual devotion. And then she had the children to raise, and they were devoted to her in her old age, perhaps even more devoted than their American counterparts would have been. When her eldest son brought a bride back to the family home, the mother's stature grew considerably, for now she too had someone to boss and to scold, someone to serve her and to gratify her ego, even as she had done for her own mother-in-law years before. She found a measure of satisfaction in playing the traditional game of butter up and trample down.

In one sense, this was—and still is—the bad age for Japanese women: their forties and fifties, when they become mothers-in-law. When they pass forty, few of them make any serious effort to retain their attractiveness or to retard the inroads of time. Why should they? It is now, if ever, that their husbands will begin to enjoy enough extra income to acquire mistresses or at least to have occasional extra-marital romances. Their husbands are seldom home, and the other children have moved away. Only the eldest son and his bride remain. What better way to spend the now-empty hours of the day than by passing on to her son's wife the same treatment she got from her own mother-in-law?

Unkempt and uncaring, her tongue grows sharp, her patience thin, and her temper short. In a word, she becomes a shrew.

But this time too passes. Either the daughter-in-law adjusts her ways to those of her husband's mother, the Empress Dowager figure, or she is rejected. Soon the older woman's bile empties itself. Grandchildren come along to divert and amuse her. She mellows. When her husband relinquishes control of family affairs to the eldest son, they both begin to enjoy life. They may move to a smaller house within the same compound, where they relax and drink tea and sun themselves and play with their grandchildren. These are their golden years.

To what extent has all this changed during the post-war years?

First and foremost were the legal changes inspired by the Supreme Commander, Allied Powers. These gave the Japanese woman rights, whereas all she had possessed previously had been duties. She was given an interest in part of her husband's property, whereas before all that she could take out of a marriage was what she had brought to it as property in her own name. (And her husband had the legal right to manage even that during the term of their marriage.) She could not now be cast aside as easily as before. As a popular saying had it, two things became stronger after the war: stockings and women.

She was also given the right to vote. Our Occupation spared her what her American sisters had to go through to acquire the franchise; Douglas MacArthur handed it to her on a silver *o-bon*. In 1946, thirty-nine women were elected to the national Diet, where there had never been even one before. Nor did the fact that many female voters had mistakenly believed that they could only cast their votes for women diminish her triumph.

The downhill road that had reached its nadir when most women were brow-beaten into wearing the wartime *mompe*—drab, baggy trousers that are the most unfeminine and most unfashionable of all conceivable garments for women—was at last beginning to slant upward. The subdued, withdrawn, melancholy women of former days now began to take hope. Little by little, as the wretched years of the early post-war era passed, they began to hold their heads up, to smile, to speak less diffidently, to think that even they themselves might hope for a measure of fulfillment as human beings.

Instead of being urged by their government to produce children every season, like animals in the field, they were pleasantly startled to be told that they should practice birth control. Coeducation was introduced, and more girls began to get higher educations. (At this writing, twenty-one percent of Japanese college students are female, in comparison to thirty-eight percent in the U.S. However, in the leading universities of Japan, the percentage is only six, while in the junior colleges, it ranges as high as sixty.)

More women began to take jobs (one out of three employed workers is female), although their pay still averages only about half that of men. They have begun to organize themselves into political, religious, and economic groupings, while their collective voices are heeded to an extent undreamed of in pre-war days. The old saw, *Fushō fuzui* (When the husband beckons, the wife had better jump), has been reversed in meaning by wags because, with fitting coincidence, the combined-form readings of the characters for husband and wife are both *fu* and can be reversed for the sake of the pun.

One of the most vivid indications of how far things have gone in the other direction is contained in a recent announcement from the Superintendence Bureau of the Japan National Railways: During the three-month period under report, fifty-three percent of those persons committing indecent acts on trains were women. (In Japan, the trains are so crowded—even standing room is at a premium during rush hours—that some men get part of their daily erotic satisfaction from pressing themselves up against the women standing next to them. If they did not like it, there was little the women could do about it, since making a scene was out of the question. Now, however, we see some of them becoming the aggressors and repaying their tormentors of the past in the same coin.—When considering the implications of this statistic, however, one should bear in mind that such "indecent acts" by men are doubtless so commonplace that many go unreported.)

As they began to understand the enlarged dimensions of their freedom, the younger women started to look around and consider what they might do, other than get married. (They had a saying: *Kekkon wa josei no hakaba de aru* or Marriage is a woman's grave.) Jobs as stage and movie actresses had always held their charm, although understandably opposed by concerned parents, but the most-desired professions became those of airline stewardesses, fashion models, and ballet dancers.

These professions, however, are admittedly not typical

of post-bellum Japanese womanhood. What then is the situation today?

The practice of *jinshin baibai* (trafficking in human flesh) remains in periodical evidence. Young girls, some mere children, flow into the two largest cities from the country districts during seasons of poor harvests and natural disasters to be caught on the hooks of the *yakuza* (gangsters) who await them in the railroad stations of Tokyo and Osaka. The methods of the dealers and the market prices may vary, but the lure of the big city and the desire to leave farm drudgery do not. And only too often their parents give them a nudge in that direction.

City maids are still working twelve hours a day, on the average. Some middle schools that had been integrated for both sexes are reverting to all-boy or all-girl status. About one-third of marriages are still arranged by parents, while many fall into the category of what are called delayed-registration marriages: After the religious ceremony, which has no legal binding in Japan, the couple begins to live together with the full approval of both sets of parents, but since the marriage is not registered with the ward or town office, it does not legally exist. During this period of "trial marriage," either party can change its mind, in which event there is no need to dissolve the marriage legally.

Most husbands still do not tell their wives when they think they may come home late. (According to a recent survey, sixty-four percent of Japanese husbands stop off "somewhere" on the way home, and within the ambiguous limits of that one word "somewhere" is contained another many-chaptered story.) Although her husband may call her by her first name (without the polite ending -*san*, of course,) the wife cannot reciprocate but must use the polite form of you (*anata*) when addressing him. When his guests come to the home (which is seldom), she is more servant than companion.

The *Shūkan Asahi*, a weekly magazine, once carried a story that says a good deal about the present situation of

Japanese women. It was an interview with the wife of the man who was Prime Minister at that time.

Madame Prime Minister told the magazine that her husband had been a rake and a womanizer in the first years of their marriage, that he had never consulted her about anything, and that he had beaten her more than a few times. (That such an interview was printed at all, however, argues for some degree of emancipation of Japanese women.)

Shortly thereafter, other reporters cornered the Prime Minister as he was leaving the Diet Building and asked him if it was true that he had beaten his wife.

Certainly it was true, he answered.

Do you still beat her? they asked.

No, not any longer, he replied, a wistful, far-off look in his eyes.

Then, in a moment of mutual male candor, he asked them, How many of *you* beat your wives nowadays?

Sheepishly, fully half of them answered that they did.

In Japan, less than one percent of newspaper reporters are women. No city mayor wears skirts. More than 90 percent of all judges are men. Only two women have been cabinet ministers in the past thirty-seven years. Tokyo University has only one female professor.

Because of figures like these, Ms. Yayori Matsui, an *Asahi* newspaper staff editor who specializes in the affairs of her sex, is of the opinion that Japan, in its treatment of the fairer sex, is one of the most backward countries in the world, only the Arab nations ranking lower.

Ms. Matsui further theorizes that an important factor in Japan's phenomenal growth is its (mis)treatment of women, who, as workers, are underpaid and exploited, while corporations bitterly resist paying them their due until forced to do so by direct court order.

At home, these women are what Ms. Matsui charac-terizes as "house slaves" and "sex slaves," serving their husbands who can then devote themselves more whole–

heartedly to their companies' prosperity, at the expense of a wholesome family life.

This chapter will close with a brief note about one of Japan's best-known women, Mrs. Fuji Murayama. Her father was co-founder of the *Asahi Shimbun*, one of the three most influential newspapers in Japan and one of the largest-circulation dailies in the world. Having no male heirs to whom he could leave his forture, Mr. Murayama adopted a son, who then married his daughter and took the family name.

Perhaps with an early inkling of his daughter's spirit of independence, however, Mr. Murayama took steps before he died to place safeguards around the editorial policies of his newspaper so that his heirs could not inject too much personal opinion and individual fancy into its editorial pages.

Nevertheless, his daughter was strong-minded enough to try to do just that in later years, and this led to a series of disputes with the editors that culminated in a court battle.

About this time, the nation was watching with half-held breath the progress of the *Asahi*-sponsored Japanese Antarctic Expedition. Everyone was extremely concerned when the expedition radioed back to Japan that its advance party was in trouble and might have to abandon their sled dogs in order to get the men back safely.

In a memorable effort—and one that will always endear her to me—to save those dogs in a civilization—and a world—where animals generally get poor treatment, Mrs. Murayama commanded the editors of the *Asahi* to radio orders to the expedition to save the dogs and, if necessary, abandon the men.

The dogs eventually *were* abandoned, and when the expedition returned to the Antarctic the following season, they found one of the animals still living. Evidently it had kept itself alive during the hard Antarctic winter by eating the others.

A New Breed
of People

One hot summer day shortly after the end of the war, we were driving south over a pitted dirt road in Kyushu, trying to find our way to Kumamoto. As we were leaving the town of Kurume, I stopped the jeep while one of the other two Americans with me asked a girl in kimono which road we should take. She did not know but obligingly offered to take us to her house nearby, where she promised to inquire of her father: a Japanese diplomat in enforced inactivity because of the war. He proved to be quite friendly and hospitable and suggested we pass an hour or so of the sweltering afternoon with him drinking beer.

The thought of anything cold to drink in that heat would have easily persuaded the three of us to accept his invitation, but actually no such persuasion was necessary. One look at our eighteen-year-old girl guide had been enough to convince us that few prices would have been too high to pay for the privilege of remaining in her vicinity even a short while longer. She was exquisitely, ineffably beautiful. Her face, her skin, her eyes, and her figure combined to form a sheer, unexampled loveliness. She was a Eurasian.

By lucky coincidence, she had two sisters, almost as pretty, so her semi-retired diplomat-father did not have to wait long for an affirmative answer when he further suggested, after two rounds of beer, that we abandon our projected weekend pleasure trip to Kumamoto and pass Saturday and Sunday in his home. After accepting, we were introduced to his French wife, whom he had met and married while assigned to the Japanese Embassy in Paris.

I wish I could report that the three of us courted and married those three Eurasian girls and lived happily ever after, but the plain truth is that we never saw them again after what was a most pleasant weekend in their Kurume home. All of us kept intending to go back, but soon thereafter I was given eight weekends of O.D. duty as punishment for a fracas I was involved in with two churlish Marine M.P.'s, and as that two-month period was ending, one of my two friends was hospitalized for exposure and exhaustion after his sailboat overturned in Hakata Bay. And so it went. Anyway, I mention the Kurume weekend because those three French-Japanese girls were the first Eurasians I met in Japan and because they, with all their beauty and charm, have always typified Eurasians for me.

Children of Japanese-European or Japanese-American unions were rare in pre-war Japan, especially in comparison to the more numerous Anglo-Indians of India and the half-Dutch Eurasians of Indonesia. Because their number was small, they were curiosities, and it has always been difficult to be a curiosity in Japan. (After Commodore Perry's 'Black Ships' visited Japan in 1854, a number of fair children were born, as might be expected. What might not have been expected was that all of them disappeared from official records and the pages of history, leaving the suspicion in the minds of many that the Japanese distaste for such racial intrusions was such that these children were not permitted to live long.)

An example of the tragedy that can befall these mixed bloods is the case of a young man with a Japanese father and English mother. Like many Eurasians, he was never allowed—by the community around him—to feel that he really belonged to either of his parents' countries, but when war with the anti-Axis powers began to appear inevitable, he had to make a choice. At first he opted to go to England, to live there, and, if called on, to fight in its forces, but when his English mother changed her mind and elected to remain at the side of her Japanese husband, she was finally able to persuade her son to stay with them. Later during the war he was drafted into the Japanese Air Force and trained as a fighter pilot. Although his first inclination had been to fight for a country that was now one of his enemies, he managed to stifle the memory of this preference and prepared to do his duty by the Rising Sun flag under which he was now serving.

The war was nearing its end by the time he completed his flight training and was assigned to a fighter squadron based in the home islands. His first two patrol flights were uneventful, but his third sortie was against a flight of attacking American B–29's. The critical shortage of spare parts rendered his Zero a less efficient fighter craft than it would otherwise have been, and he was shot down in flames during his second pass at the underbelly of one of the enemy bombers.

Parachuting out of the Zero, the Eurasian pilot found that he was wounded in the shoulder and that his flight suit was on fire in three places. While floating earthward, he succeeded in extinguishing the flames but sustained painful burns in so doing. Off to his right, he chanced to see one of the B–29's going down in flames and two parachutes suddenly blossom near it.

The Eurasian hit the ground hard and lay there under the folds of his parachute momentarily stunned. In a few minutes, however, he staggered to his feet and struggled out of both his parachute and badly-charred flight suit. Clad only in his underwear, he started to stumble scross the fields toward a road visible in the distance but half-way there he collapsed and fainted from loss of blood and the pain of his burns and bullet wound.

Japanese farmers found him where he lay. Seeing his

somewhat foreign features, they assumed that he was one of the Americans who had jumped from the burning B–29. They beat him to death with shovels.

A Eurasian friend of mine once told me about an experience of his that, while far less tragic than the one above, at least illustrates another problem faced by some children of mixed marriages. Lou, which was the name my friend took in later years when he worked for an American company, was born in Germany of a Japanese father and a German mother and was raised and educated in Berlin. His parents took him to Japan with them a few months before the Pearl Harbor attack, when Lou was nineteen. Although he was able to speak Japanese, he had absolutely no knowledge of the written language, but this made no difference the following year when he was drafted into the Japanese army.

Lou was tall for a Japanese and impressive in appearance. A scar on his left cheek and a trim moustache added years to his face, the features of which were more Japanese than European. After being inducted, Lou was sent to a training camp where he was assigned to a tent and told to await the return of his company, which would be gone until the following day on a field exercise. That evening Lou decided to take a bath, so in his underwear and *geta* he went nosing through the camp until he found a tent within which were placed several large wooden tubs filled with steaming water and five or six bathers. Paying no heed to the sign at the entrance—which he could not read, Lou entered briskly through the tent-flap and found a place for himself in one of the tubs.

In the naked camaraderie of the bath, the Japanese bathers greeted Lou readily enough, then resumed their conversation about the news of the fighting on Guadalcanal. Most of them left the bath in a group about ten minutes later, after bowing and politely saying goodnight to Lou.

The next day the Eurasian recruit, dressed in his new private's uniform, was walking to the message center to mail a letter when he chanced to meet one of the bathers of the night before—dressed in the uniform of a major. Recognizing Lou immediately, the major flew into an explosive rage. Screaming insults and threats, he beat the startled private severely about the head and shoulders with the flat of his sword until his arm gave out. Then he led Lou off to his company commander to demand still further punishment.

The sign at the entrance to the bath-tent that Lou had been unable to read had said, of course, that this particular bath was reserved for field-grade officers. Unable to imagine any enlisted man with the temerity to enter their tent, the majors and colonels with whom Lou had pleasantly passed the time side by side in the wooden tubs had accepted him as a visiting officer of field-grade rank. That he might not have been able to read the sign in a country with the highest literacy rate in the world did not occur to them.

Estimates of the number of Eurasian (or, more accurately, Amerasian) children that Americans have fathered in Japan since the end of the war range from five thousand to fifty thousand and even higher. Pearl Buck, a distinguished woman of letters and a compassionate human being who devoted much of her time and money to the plight of Amerasian orphans in Asia, wrote that by conservative estimate one in every ten American men stationed in the Far East since 1945 has fathered a half-caste child.

Japan has no reliable statistics on the number of *konketsuji* (lit., mixed-blood children) within her borders. These children do not become the objects of statistical interest until they enter orphan homes or entangle themselves with the police. But whether they number ten thousand or one hundred thousand, they are *our* responsibility. We American men who fought and worked—and wooed—in Asia are the ones responsible for the presence on earth of these hapless, innocent children.

Not all of us, of course. But the children are there in irrefutable proof that some among us gave them life. Can we afford to shrug it off and say that it must have been the other fellow? Almost any among us, except Kipling's plaster saints, may be guilty. I may be. If you are a man and if you were there, you too may be. We may never know.

Twenty-two-year old Kazuko Kitayama is the Amerasian daughter of an American Negro soldier and a Japanese woman. Presumably, her father does not know that Kazuko exists. He was invited to visit the home of Kazuko's mother and the Japanese man to whom she was married one night not long after the beginning of the Occupation. He had too much to drink and took advantage of the husband's absence from the house on emergency business to rape his hostess. Overcome with shame, she could not bring herself to tell her husband what had happened. Later, when she knew that she was pregnant, she prayed that the baby's father was her husband and not their black visitor, whom they never saw again. Her prayers failed. The baby was obviously part Negro. Although her husband did not reproach her, she became like a woman possessed, continually begging for his forgiveness. This he readily gave, but her guilt—and his imagined umbrage— had become for her an idee fixe. Unable to stomach food, she went into a decline and died soon thereafter.

Her husband loved the baby girl Kazuko and cared for her as best he could until he too died eleven years later. Without his protection, Kazuko was then fully exposed to the harsh realities of a society where Amerasian children were seldom accepted. Especially not when they have Negro blood and their mothers were presumed to have been unfaithful wives. Japanese children often call Amerasians like Kazuko *kurombō* (niggers) and *hitokui jinshu* (cannibals). She grew up hating her unknown father and the darkness of her skin. Many times in the bath she would scrub herself with a stiff brush until droplets of blood oozed out through her pores in a childish, furious urge to lighten her color.

But, as if in realization that this miserable child was nearing a breaking point, fortune at last turned the other side of its face toward Kazuko. She was given a chance to learn to sing under the tutelage of a famous songstress, Sanae Mizushima. Then she became nationally popular when she recorded *The Needle*, a song dedicated to the restoration of peace in Viet Nam.

Nowadays other Amerasians like Kazuko Kitayama are becoming famous and, in a few cases, rich. Michi Aoyama is an example. Michi's fame as a singer helped in her long search for her father. She found him in Texas, with his American wife and children. Still other Amerasians have become well-known fashion models, M.C.'s, and actors and actresses. One (really a *Eur*asian) became Japan's leading sumo wrestler: the greatest in the history of the centuries-old sport.

The undeniable physical attractiveness with which many Amerasians and Eurasians are blessed (perhaps in partial compensation for the hard lot fate has handed them) has eased their way into the movies and onto the stage. Their Oriental blood softens the sometimes harsh features inherited from the West, while our blood relieves the comparative flatness of Oriental faces. Pearl Buck has called them "a new breed of people who can be the strongest, most beautiful, and most intelligent in history. . . ." She suggests survival of the fittest as a reason for this superiority: Half of these mixed blood children die before they reach the age of five because of the neglect and poverty in which they are raised.

The number of Amerasians who have found fame and comparative affluence in the entertainment and fashion worlds, however, is a pitifully small percentage of the total. Most of the others are poor, ill-educated, and mistreated by the society in which they must live. True or not, they are usually assumed to be the illegitimate offspring of prostitute mothers and cruel, low-class fathers, which only increases the hostility with which the surrounding society views them. They are strangers in their own world, strangers who have no home to which they can ever return.

They do not understand why the world does not accept them. Nor do I. Not really. I am familiar enough with some of the explanations, like what certain Japanese said reproachfully to Mrs. Miki Sawada when she started her home for Amerasian orphans in Japan: "Why do you bother to help them? Their fathers are the ones who dropped the atom bomb on Hiroshima, aren't they?" Although I know of this and other explanations, I am unable to comprehend such cruelty in human beings. I know that it must be there, but the concept appalls me, and I shrink from it in revulsion.

In addition to the thousands of Amerasians in Japan, there are many more elsewhere in the Far East. In Okinawa. In the Philippines. In Korea. In Thailand. And in Viet Nam.

More than forty thousand live—or at least survive—in Korea, with five or six hundred more being born every year. Annie Park was one of these. When she was only six, she witnessed her Korean mother in the act of selling her body to an American soldier. Immediately, in a state of semishock, Annie ran out into the night, only to be lured into an alley and assaulted. By the time she was sixteen, Annie had become a full-time hooker catering to American servicemen. By the age of nineteen, she had prostituted herself to thousands of Americans and had undergone six abortions. Annie Park's case is exceptional—but only because she wrote a book telling what had happened to her, and the book, with all its lurid details, became a best-seller. (Its title was *My Forsaken Star.*)

There are only too many other Annie Parks whose stories may never be known. Do we, as a people, really care to know them, to concern ourselves with the miseries of these young people?

It is only natural for these youngsters to tend to completely identify themselves with either their mother's or their father's country. Having no fathers and living, for example, in Japan, many would understandably like to become fully-accepted Japanese, but the Japanese themselves will not allow that. In their bitter despair and frustration, some Amerasians resort to extremes.

Once a sixteen-year-old boy of Japanese-Negro parentage raped and strangled three young women in Japan. When caught and interrogated by the police, he would say only, "I did it because I hate my kinky hair and the color of my skin."

There are good reasons (human decency, responsibility, compassion, among others) why we should help these Amerasian children. If we do not, they may easily turn to crime—or to Communism. Their tattered presence in Asia will always serve to remind the Japanese, Koreans, Vietnamese, and other Orientals that we Americans have abandoned our own offspring. While we spend billions of dollars and many long years supporting, for example, the Chinese Nationalist regime on Taiwan mainly to prove to the people of Asia that we abide by our commitments, we are destroying the impression we have been trying to create by callously ignoring the children our men have fathered and forgotten throughout the Far East. And yet we could save them by the expenditure of only a small fraction of the money we have spent on the behalf of Taiwan.

Until recently these Amerasians were all children, mostly tucked away out of sight in orphanages or running wild and hungry in slum districts that Americans seldom visit. But more and more, as they become men and women, they will be seen and heard. To a large extent, we still have the power, if we act now, to influence whether these "forgotten mementoes of our momentary passions" become leaders of decent society or leaders of Communist cells or leaders of criminal gangs.

Or simply ill-used, wretched outcasts.

194 Tokugawa era ends in 1868, year of the Meiji Re-storation
208 the Heian Period (794–1185)
210 the Muromachi Era (1392–1573)

TRAVEL AND CULTURE BOOKS

"World at Its Best" Travel Series
Britain, France, Germany, Hawaii,
Holland, Hong Kong, Italy, Spain,
Switzerland, London, New York, Paris,
Washington, D.C., San Francisco

Passport's Travel Guides and References
IHT Guides to Business Travel in Asia &
Europe
Only in New York
Mystery Reader's Walking Guides:
London, England, New York, Chicago
Chicago's Best-Kept Secrets
London's Best-Kept Secrets
New York's Best-Kept Secrets
The Japan Encyclopedia
Japan Today!
Japan at Night
Japan Made Easy
Discovering Cultural Japan
Living in Mexico
The Hispanic Way
Guide to Ethnic Chicago
Guide to Ethnic London
Guide to Ethnic New York
Guide to Ethnic Montreal
Passport's Trip Planner & Travel Diary
Chinese Etiquette and Ethics in Business
Korean Etiquette and Ethics in Business
Japanese Etiquette and Ethics in Business
How to Do Business with the Japanese
Japanese Cultural Encounters
The Japanese

Passport's Regional Guides of France
Auvergne, Provence, Loire Valley,
Dordogne & Lot, Languedoc, Brittany, South
West France, Normandy & North West
France, Paris, Rhône Valley & Savoy,
France for the Gourmet Traveler

Passport's Regional Guides of Indonesia
New Guinea, Java, Borneo, Bali, East of
Bali, Sumatra, Spice Islands,
Sulawesi, Exploring the Islands of
Indonesia

Up-Close Guides
Paris, London, Manhattan, Amsterdam,
Rome

Passport's "Ticket To..." Series
Italy, Germany, France, Spain

**Passport's Guides: Asia, Africa, Latin
America, Europe, Middle East**
Japan, Korea, Malaysia, Singapore, Bali,
Burma, Australia, New Zealand, Egypt,
Kenya, Philippines, Portugal, Moscow,
St. Petersburg, The Georgian Republic,
Mexico, Vietnam, Iran, Berlin, Turkey

Passport's China Guides
All China, Beijing, Fujian, Guilin,
Hangzhou & Zhejiang, Hong Kong,
Macau, Nanjing & Jiangsu, Shanghai,
The Silk Road, Taiwan, Tibet, Xi'an,
The Yangzi River, Yunnan

Passport's India Guides
All India; Bombay & Goa; Dehli, Agra
& Jaipur; Burma; Pakistan;
Kathmandu Valley; Bhutan; Museums
of India; Hill Stations of India

Passport's Thai Guides
Bangkok, Phuket, Chiang Mai, Koh Sumi

On Your Own Series
Brazil, Israel

"Everything Under the Sun" Series
Spain, Barcelona, Toledo, Seville,
Marbella, Cordoba, Granada, Madrid,
Salamanca, Palma de Majorca

Passport's Travel Paks
Britain, France, Italy, Germany, Spain

Exploring Rural Europe Series
England & Wales, France, Greece,
Ireland, Italy, Spain, Austria,
Germany, Scotland, Ireland by Bicycle

Regional Guides of Italy
Florence & Tuscany, Naples & Campania,
Umbria, the Marches & San Marino

Passport Maps
Europe, Britain, France, Italy, Holland,
Belgium & Luxembourg, Scandinavia,
Spain & Portugal, Switzerland, Austria
& the Alps

Passport's Trip Planners & Guides
California, France, Greece, Italy

PASSPORT BOOKS
a division of *NTC Publishing Group*
Lincolnwood, Illinois USA